To Linda
 You make such a difference
in the lives of SO many

 May God bless you as
you live your life blessing
others

 The Joy of the Lord
 is our strength

 Carole Myrick
 407.340.7551

June 20, 2011
RE: *Escape Under The Kenyan Moon*

I first read an earlier draft of Carole Myrick's work several years ago. I had known Carole during those difficult years of her marriage to the son of an African tribal chief, and kept in touch with her after her escape back to the U.S. Her personal and sensitive account of her years married to Otieno Habembe moved me more than I could have expected, given that I personally knew much of her story.

The final draft of *Escape Under The Kenyan Moon* includes so much more than that earlier draft. Her years of reflection on the meaning of that traumatic yet miraculous period in her life and the lives of her children have given the text a clearer sense of what it all meant to the four of them.

As a retired pastor, I have experienced many "missionary stories" over my career. Some have stirred me, some inspired me, some disappointed me a bit, and others left questions in my mind that I could not answer. In *Escape Under The Kenyan Moon,* Carole seems to have achieved that delicate balance between narrative, strong personal emotions, faith under fire, and the miracle working power of missionaries in a divine place at a divine moment. I believe those who have any love for such mission-based stories will find this book compelling, exciting, authentic, and inspiring.

My 30 years in public library work (prior to my pastoral career) helps me predict that many who read the blurb of this book will decide to buy it. I also imagine that the story could be a solid choice for a made-for-TV movie on one of the women's cable channels. I can imagine the long-term effect the "spider" scene in the hut on the island in Lake Victoria could have on viewers of every age!

Wallace W. White
Delaware, OH
wallaceww@juno.com

# ESCAPE UNDER THE KENYAN MOON

*A True Story By*

CAROLE MYRICK

Askari Publishing, LLC books may be ordered through booksellers or by contacting:

Askari Publishing, LLC
PO Box 616278
Orlando, FL 32861
www.escapeunderthekenyanmoon.com
1-(407) 521-0104

ISBN-13: 978-1491291955
ISBN-10: 1491291958

Library of Congress Control Number: 2012923040
Printed in the United States of America

Rev. date: 12/12/2012

# ESCAPE UNDER THE KENYAN MOON

A true story by
Carole Myrick.

To
## Dan & Cathy Schellenberg
For showing me the living meaning of love

*Greater love has no one than this, that he lay down his life for his friends.*

JOHN 15:13
New International Version

# Contents

# CHAPTER 1: AMERICA

## *Rock Me Gently*

**March 10ᵗʰ 1982:**

It was quiet and dark. Most of the passengers on the plane were asleep. Four-year-old Otiga and three-year-old Nekessa slept on blankets beneath my seat, while their ten-year-old sister, Melissa, curled up next to me. My mind whirled with images from the past forty-eight hours. We had escaped and we were flying home after almost two years in Kenya. But what were we going home to? I had three small children, no husband, no money, no job, and no possessions except for the few things I'd thrown into two suitcases at the last minute.

I checked on the children. They looked so peaceful, so unaware of the dangers they had just lived through. "Thank you, Lord." I still couldn't believe we had escaped! A question kept darting in and out of my mind, making it impossible to sleep; how did I get into this nightmare. I had a long time to consider this because we had thousands of miles yet to travel. The story unfolded in my head as I struggled to put the pieces together.

**Preface:**

As far back as I can remember, my goal was to please my parents. Growing up in the small town of Marion, Ohio, during the 1950's and 1960's made this job easier. In high school I strived to be a model

1

daughter. I didn't smoke, drink, or rebel. I even earned a scholarship to Ohio State University. My father expected me to graduate from OSU and to remain a virgin until I was married. I honored both of his requests. While I was a freshman, I met Alan, a senior at Ohio State. He graduated, became a stockbroker, but he was drafted in a few months and was sent to Vietnam. Two long years later (in 1968), he returned safely from Vietnam, I graduated from Ohio State, and we were married.

We began our storybook life together in Columbus, Ohio. I was an elementary schoolteacher and Alan was a financial analyst. We had wine-tasting parties and exciting vacations but we had no time for God. I'd been raised in a Christian home and there were moments I knew that I was off track, but it was easy to let the roar of the world drown out these thoughts.

By our fourth anniversary we had a healthy baby girl named Melissa, a charming two-story brick house, a lust for the good life, and ample income to maintain this lifestyle. What else could we need? We needed God, but we were too self absorbed to realize it.

After seven years, we grew tired of each Other. We had neither taken the time nor made the effort to develop a solid foundation in our marriage. So when we experienced stormy weather, we were blown apart. We had lived the good life according to the values of the world, but this good life had undermined our marriage and deadened my senses to the truth. I was lost and confused. I knew something was missing, but I didn't know what it was or how to find it.

Alan was too civilized to argue about our problems, so we politely agreed to end our marriage. We even met for coffee before we went to court for our divorce. Looking back on it now, I realize we were probably poorly matched. He was very organized and quite unemotional. I was unorganized, naive, and bubbling over with emotion.

I was twenty-nine years old, and I had crashed on the fast lane of life. I had lived life my way and failed. I abandoned Jesus, but fortunately He hadn't abandoned me. After many months of trying to heal my own emotional wounds, I joined a Baptist church recommended by my brother, Graham, who was in seminary at this time. It's easier to hear what God is saying when you are ready to listen. Life began to make sense. At least that's what I thought.

## The Story, 1976:

My journey began with two words, Otieno Habembe. I would never erase the sound of his voice nor alter the events that set this life changing adventure into motion, even with all the pain that was woven into the tapestry of our lives.

Otieno came from Uganda, East Africa, to study food science and nutrition at Ohio State University. He was given a full scholarship by the United Nations' Food and Agricultural Organization (FAO).

Otieno grew up on Sigulu Island, a primitive island in the middle of Lake Victoria in East Africa. The village was small and isolated. There was no running water or electricity. A mud hut with a grass thatched roof was his home. The outside world seldom intruded, except for an occasional missionary. Leaving this island for an education in the United States was an unprecedented accomplishment. After graduation, he would be required to return to Uganda to continue his work in the quality control of milk production.

Otieno was the last born child of his mother, Auma. His father, Habembe, was the chief of the village, and was considered wealthy, because he owned five wives and many sheep and goats. As a young boy, he slept on a mat along with the chickens, in his mother's one-room mud hut, except on the nights his father came to visit. On those occasions, he was sent to another wife's hut. Each wife had her own hut, and Habembe stayed with each one on a rotating basis.

One of Otieno's favorite games as a child was running and challenging the other boys in some test of strength or skill (much like any boy in any country). They played soccer with a ball made of rags and string. When he was very young, he began accompanying his father and his uncles on their all-night fishing trips on Lake Victoria. When he became a teenager, he had to build his own hut because he was now considered a man.

Because Otieno was the last-born son, and he was an exceptionally intelligent child, he was given an education beyond the limited schooling of the island. His older brother, Otiga, made it financially possible for him to attend the University in Uganda. This opened the door for Otieno to further his education in America.

The first time our worlds collided was at an international event while he was at Ohio State University. Otieno had the commanding presence of a natural leader. He appeared younger than his thirty-three years, and his aura shouted confidence, excitement and charm. His body was trim and muscular, with skin like polished ebony that fit tightly across his broad shoulders and strong arms. He had a passion for life that energized everything he did. I also had an energizing passion for life which may have been the force that drew us to each other.

Although Otieno spent many years away from the island studying food science and nutrition, his true love was fishing. Because food in most of Africa was not always plentiful, fish was a very important part of his diet. He believed his family was very fortunate because they had fish to eat, unlike the inland tribes.

One evening while we were having dinner at a seafood restaurant, Otieno was sharing his memories of growing up on the island. He missed the dried fish he ate as a boy. This small fish was sun-dried whole, and was very salty and crisp. It sounded a lot like fish jerky to me. Unfortunately, the restaurant had never heard of it, so he ordered broiled fish. I guess you just couldn't get good fish jerky in America.

As I ordered my favorite seafood, shrimp, horror spread across Otieno's face. I immediately looked around the restaurant to see if it was on fire. His voice reeked with disgust as he asked, "What are you doing? You can't order that rubbish! We use shrimp for bait. They eat the garbage off the bottom of the lake. There's no way you can put that trash in your mouth."

I had just crashed head-on into a cultural wall. "But I love shrimp and lobster." I argued. The waitress seemed a little anxious as she looked at me and then at Otieno. Her expression suggested that someone needed to order! I didn't feel this was the right time to do battle, so I gave in and ordered broiled fish also.

As we lingered over our dinner, he calmed down and we were able to talk quietly about shrimp, lobster, and the many differences arising from our diverse cultures.

During the evening, I reminded myself that Otieno and I were just friends. However the magnetism drawing us together from our opposite worlds was overpowering. I was twenty-nine years old, so this could not be explained as a school girl crush. There were times when I wondered if I was under the spell of some ancient magic that flowed from his piercing black eyes.

Before the night was over, we came to a friendly compromise. Otieno would never eat shrimp or lobster, and although shrimp was a cultural taboo for him, he wouldn't ask me to stop eating it. We had successfully broken through a few bricks in the cultural wall between us, at least for the evening.

Every time we were together, Otieno mesmerized me with stories about his childhood on the island. The first time he saw a white person he was terrified because he thought someone had stripped off the man's skin, leaving only the light-colored flesh underneath. When he was just a child playing on the beach, away from the cover of the plush tropical vegetation, he saw the vapor trail of a jet airplane and thought it was a giant snake crawling across the sky.

Otieno had been exposed to Catholicism when he was young, but it was fear of the local black magic that held him captive. He always carried a small black pouch containing the end of a rhinoceros horn that was filled with a fine black powder. He rubbed this powder into cuts that were made in his skin with a special razor, which was also kept in the pouch. He had a series of scars, always three in a row, on his body, resulting from this tribal custom. He would never tell me what the powder was or why he did this to himself. He would merely lock eyes with me and answer matter-of-factly, "It's one of our tribal traditions." He smiled a large toothy grin as he shared another custom. He was the first son from the village who didn't have his two front teeth removed.

One evening as we were out dancing, I asked myself, "Why are you acting like this? You're hurting your parents." It was true. My parents were furious with me. All the years of being a model daughter were disregarded. I had committed an unpardonable sin in their eyes, and I could not be forgiven unless I gave up this unacceptable relationship. I had always tried to please my parents, but this time I was not willing to obey them.

As my body moved with his to the tune of "Rock Me Gently" by Andy Kim, the words flooded my mind.

> Rock me gently
> Rock me slowly
> Take it easy
> Don't you know
> That I have never been loved like this before.

This was true. I had never felt loved the way I felt with him. I was deaf and blind to all advice concerning the perceived problems of our relationship.

The question of color was never an issue for either of us, but it brought constant stares and often hateful comments from strangers. The picture of a very black man with a petite, blonde and blue eyed Caucasian woman enraged many people during the 1970's. We had to be careful where we went together in public. This was also a major concern for my parents. They were furious with me! If it had been anyone else, I would have submitted to their demands.

It was inevitable that Otieno and I would be married, and it was also inevitable that this marriage would explode like a grenade, shattering my family into fragments. "You can't do this," screamed my mother over the phone. "Why can't you see what you are doing to your family?

I won't be a part of this, Carole, and you won't be a part of our lives if you go through with this marriage."

Tears welled up inside and escaped from under my closed eyelids. She was right; I was disobeying and hurting them. I ached all over because I didn't want to cause them this pain. I loved them, and I had always tried to please them; but this time I couldn't. Why were they unable to understand? I was glad the anger had been filtered through the phone cables. It would have been unbearable to hear these words in person, and to see the anger and pain clouding over her once-loving eyes. Did she really mean I could no longer be part of our family? I couldn't imagine the void that would exist in my life without them.

Then I thought about the alternative; life without Otieno. What magical power did he have over me that I would choose to be disowned by my family rather than live without him? I knew my parents were responding this way because they loved me and wanted what they believed was best for me. Was my attraction to him a rebound from my marriage to Alan, who was very civilized, and quite unemotional? Otieno was like the negative of a photograph of Alan, exactly the opposite in every way. I laughed at the thought of this comparison. It was true.

Otieno was an intriguing mixture of primitive and civilized cultures. He moved and spoke with the confidence of a king. His deep dark voice was enhanced by his captivating British-African accent. It was like listening to thunder wrapped in a tuxedo. His face seemed to be carved out of ebony, accentuating his strong high cheekbones and brooding eyebrows. But his eyes were the most electrifying feature. The power in those cold black spheres cut straight into my heart and removed it so that it belonged only to him.

I saw in him a passion for life that excited me, and at the same time a raging fire that frightened me. If I had listened to my head, I would have run from him, but my heart filled a larger part of me, so my head seldom won the battles. I would attempt to plead my case before my parents, but I knew our relationship had already been tried and condemned and there would be no appealing it.

Some months earlier, Otieno joined the church I was attending and he had accepted Jesus as his Savior. We were attending marriage counseling classes with our Pastor, and he was meeting with him for counseling as a new Christian. Because Otieno and I came from different cultures, we combined both customs in our ceremony. We wrote our marriage vows under the guidance of our pastor. We agreed that the actual wedding vows were to honor the traditional Christian commitment of a monogamous marriage, one husband and one wife with God as the center and head of our family.

Otieno Habembe and I were married on August 28, 1976. The only family members present at our wedding were Melissa and my brother, Fred. My best friend June was the maid of honor. Unlike me, her head had more power over her decisions, so she also had doubts about my unconventional marriage. Being a true friend, she shared her concerns, but when our vows were spoken, she was standing beside me. It was an unusual wedding. The groom's dress was more stunning than mine.

He wore a brightly colored African robe, and I wore a cream-colored floor length dress. As we dedicated our lives to each other, the sky opened and drenched the earth. This was a blessing in his society. However, the shadows of my absent family dampened the joy of this celebration. Fred tried to ease the void of my missing parents and my brother Graham, but there were still gaping holes of sadness that could be filled by no one else.

The beauty of our wedding flowed into the pleasure of our honeymoon. Otieno introduced me to feelings I had never known existed, unlocking the woman in me that was ready to be set free.

I quickly discovered that life with Otieno would never be normal. As soon as we were married, I added him to my auto insurance. My policy was immediately cancelled. It seemed that he drove in America the same way they drove in Uganda, fast and faster! Unfortunately this just wasn't acceptable here, so we had to go on a high-risk policy that cost twice as much as the original policy.

Meals were never the same again. Chicken gizzards suddenly became a status symbol to be served to the most important male guest in the house. Cream of wheat was no longer served at breakfast, but was now cooked into a solid gooey ball, called ugali, torn into pieces, and dunked into a broth for supper. I learned to cook many new dishes that I knew I must grow to love.

A few months after we were married I received a phone call from my dentist, reminding me of my six-month appointment to have my teeth cleaned and checked. While the receptionist was on the phone, I asked Otieno if he wanted me to schedule an appointment for him. "An appointment for what?" he asked innocently." I've never been to a dentist."

I was a little stunned, but with Otieno this happened often. I knew he brushed his teeth, and he had a bright smile. How could he be in his thirties and never have been to a dentist? I immediately scheduled an appointment for him, hoping it wasn't too late to save his teeth. I felt sorry for him because he hadn't had the medical and dental care I took for granted. He didn't seem disturbed about this at all. He obviously didn't understand the importance of professional care.

However, he did understand how he had been taught to care for his teeth in his family. He had a small wooden stick about the width and length of a pencil broken in half. The broken end was flattened down and smooth. He used this stick to polish his teeth by rubbing the end of it around every tooth for quite a long time. A broken stick? He used an old broken stick to clean his teeth! Oh, well, he would quickly learn the correct way to care for his teeth. It was good he had me to help him with these unfamiliar subjects.

I gave my appointment to Otieno so he wouldn't have to wait any longer to begin the proper dental care. I accompanied him to the dentist since this was his first time and he might feel uneasy. I had explained the situation to the dental hygienist before we arrived so she would give him special, tender loving care. She took him back to the chair, and I remained in the waiting room, worrying. How would he react to drilling, root canals, and the other horrible tortures I had experienced throughout my life? I was trying to remain brave for my husband, as the memories of my past visits to the dentist made my teeth ache. I wondered if he would even consider returning to have the dental work completed on his poor neglected teeth.

As I was fighting this mental battle for Otieno, he walked out, looking brave and confident. How could that be? He had just been through his first dental appointment. Maybe the Novocain had numbed his brain also? The dentist followed closely behind my confused husband. "How bad is it, Doctor?" I asked sympathetically.

Dr. Davis smiled at me as he shared the news. "Apparently he was taught excellent oral hygiene because he has no cavities. His teeth and gums are in excellent condition."

Otieno just continued to flash his confident smile. He had dazzled the entire staff with his strong teeth, his sexy accent, and his overflowing charm. He also taught me a valuable lesson. Civilization and all its progress, does not have all the answers! And neither did I. After I rescheduled my appointment, I went home to contemplate this confusing experience. Maybe he would make a little wooden stick for me to use on my teeth before my next appointment.

The following year, in July, our first child, Otiga Habembe was born. "He's huge, look at him!" I laughed as I examined our freshly brewed son. It had taken only about four hours for the journey from his cramped but secure quarters into this stark naked reality. Otiga had arrived just as the nine months of previews of coming attractions had predicted: large, strong, and very active. He had punched and kicked me for months. I should have known he was going to be king size. He weighed nine pounds, nine ounces, and was twenty-two inches long. He was unlike anything I had imagined. He had an excess of straight black hair. He wasn't really white, and he wasn't very black. He was huge, especially his head. But then, my body had realized this even before my eyes did.

Otieno was shouting joyous sounds in Abaluhya, his native language. I didn't know what he was saying, but I knew he was thrilled. He had accomplished the impossible for an African man. He had taken Lamaze classes with me and he had participated in Otiga's birth. I knew this wasn't a part of his traditions, but he had handled the experience like a pro. His already proud stride seemed even more confident as he carried our son to me. He spoke without moving his eyes from Otiga, "Look at my son. I wish I could take him home to my village. He will be a leader some day." His deep, powerful voice quivered with excitement. The remaining words must have been spoken only to Otiga, because he never looked up as he lowered his voice and spoke in his native language.

Otieno had wanted a son. Sons were a status symbol in his social order. He had named our son after his older brother, Otiga, who had died mysteriously soon after he had put Otieno through the university in Kenya. He had loved his brother Otiga, and this was a way to honor him. Otiga was adorable but probably only to Otieno and me. That was fine because there wouldn't be many others looking at him. My parents had decided they could not bear the humiliation of coming to the hospital and claiming a biracial baby as their grandchild. I was prepared for the rejection, or at least I thought I was; but my mind would occasionally drift back to five years ago when Melissa was born. Then, the flowers and the grandparents had left very little space for Melissa and me. It did hurt when they didn't send flowers or call to see how mother and baby were doing. However, I was determined to feel enough joy and excitement for everyone who should be happy, but wasn't.

"We're doing fine, Mom," I said in our imaginary conversation. "His eyes are so bright and alert that I almost expect him to speak. He's so big that Otieno has nicknamed him 'Jangola Kwach,' which means fierce leopard. The name fits, I'm afraid." Oh, I shouldn't have mentioned the name, Otieno. She hated the word! It's a good thing this was a make-believe conversation, or I would have been suddenly talking to myself.

I was checked into my room while Otiga was being "checked out" and cleaned up from his tiring trip through the birth canal. I was on a natural high, so it was difficult to calm down and rest. Instead, I took inventory of my room. It was comfortable. I had a roommate who was only semi-conscious because she had just undergone a C-section and hadn't completely returned to awareness. Otiga would be spending his days with me in the room and his nights in the nursery. I was anxiously awaiting his arrival when an older woman, dressed in white, appeared at our door. She had Otiga in her arms as she glanced over the occupants, and then quickly took him to the foot of my roommate's bed. Before I could interrupt her, she began the required question. "What is the number of your hospital bracelet? Please read it to me."

Cathy, the black woman in bed 301-B, responded with, "786-521."

The nurse looked upset! "That's not the number on this bracelet," she said in a very confused voice. I called to her as she re-read Otiga's bracelet, "That's my bracelet number." She came to my bed, looking no less confused, and asked me to read off my number. They matched, so I got the prize, Otiga.

I laughed after she left the room. I would have loved to have heard the story she shared at the nurse's station. I removed the soft, pastel striped blanket that was tightly wrapped around my son. I examined every finger and toe. He was such a creative combination of Otieno and me, and yet unlike either of us. I thought about his name, Otiga Habembe. It meant warrior.

He would have to be strong like a warrior to make it in this New World he had just entered. We stayed in the hospital for two more days. It was nice to have friends who tried to fill the void left by my parents, but unfortunately, family-shaped voids can never be filled completely by anything but family.

The next morning a different lady in white, somewhat preoccupied, came to the door with Otiga, and quickly surveyed the patients. With total confidence, she scurried past my bed to do the required bracelet check with the stunning black woman in the next bed. "I believe you have my baby," I said.

She looked at me en-route and confidently shook her head, "no."

With just a hint of a smile, I nodded my head, "yes," as I read my bracelet number to support my claim. She quickly deposited Otiga in my arms, and hurried on to her other duties. I began enjoying this comedy routine that occurred with some variation each time my large brown son was returned to me from the nursery.

The quiet private time in the hospital that allows a mother and baby to bond closely together was over. It had been a successful bonding. All the fears I had felt about not being able to love another child as much as I loved Melissa were dissolved. There was more than enough love for both children. It was time to go home. I checked Otiga's and my bracelets one more time, just in case. We matched – at least our bracelets did! I wondered if we should wear them for a while longer, to ease the fears of those people who wouldn't believe that he was my son. That was their problem. I knew who we were and we belonged together.

After Otiga's birth, Otieno often longed to return to his home. The Immigration Department had allowed him to remain in America and work after he graduated from Ohio State, because it would have been too dangerous for Otiga and me to go to Uganda while Idi Amin was still the dictator. He hated Americans. I knew that our time in the United States was temporary. I had accepted this in my heart. I could not expect him to stay in my country forever.

When our beautiful light brown daughter, Auma Nekessa, was born the following year, it increased Otieno's desire to return to Africa. He named our delicate little baby girl after his mother, Auma, and he dreamed of taking our little Auma home.

Raising Melissa, Otiga, and Nekessa was my greatest joy, and often provided moments of interesting dialogue with strangers. "Oh, what lovely children you have," flowed from an older woman with gray hair and a matching gray suit.

"Thank you," I modestly answered.

"Are the babies adopted?" she asked. Her smile was soft, and I could tell she was enjoying the children.

"No." I smiled back at her.

"Oh, you're a foster parent!" she exclaimed, with admiration in her voice.

"No, they're all my own children. My older daughter is Melissa, my son's name is Otiga Habembe, and my baby's name is Auma Nekessa." I searched her face for a sign. Had she understood my answer? At this point the conversation could go in one of two directions. The inquisitive woman would either become quiet and walk away, or she would ask about the strange sounding names.

"What interesting names," she cooed. "What nationality are the little ones?" I could tell she was too intrigued with Otiga and Nekessa to walk away now. I was more relaxed with the question than I had been in the past.

"They are Luhya," I answered, knowing this response would tell her absolutely nothing. This would give her one last chance to pull out of the conversation, or I would be sharing this somewhat sensitive subject with another stranger. Later that evening, I thought about her questions. I knew there would be many more people with many more questions, but we would be fine. God had created our children wonderfully, and my goal was to help others see their unique beauty.

A year later, Otieno went home to visit with his family. When he left, I knew we would be moving to Africa soon. He returned from his journey with African soil on his feet and in his heart. It was time to go home. However, because of the devastation and political massacres occurring in Uganda under Idi Amin, it was not safe for Otieno to return to Uganda with us, so he decided instead to take us almost home to neighboring Kenya.

# CHAPTER 2: KENYA

## *So Much Beauty, So Much Time*

It was difficult to believe Melissa and I were actually on a plane, leaving America and heading to our new home in Thika, Kenya. I watched her fidget in her seat as she tried to appear calm. Melissa was only eight years old, and this uprooting was painful for her. Pale and anxious, she stuttered questions between long periods of silence, as she fought back the tears. She was leaving her father, Alan, and the only way to see him again would be to travel back to America, alone. Neither of us spoke of this problem, as we sped away from her heritage. She was an experienced flier, traveling often from our home in Indiana to be with her father in Ohio. However, she understood it would not be as easy in the future. Her hazy eyes and quivering lips betrayed her, as she tried to sound brave. "Mommy, all the kids at school think it's neat I'm going to Africa. I'm not really scared that we're going, I'm just a little sad I'm leaving."

I understood what she was saying. My heart ached from the pain of leaving my family and friends, but I was excited because in less than twenty-four hours I would be reunited with my husband and my toddlers. It had been extremely difficult being left behind to finalize all the details of such a major move. However, the most trying part had been watching my almost two-year-old Nekessa, my three-year-old Otiga, and Otieno leave without knowing when Melissa and I would be able to join them.

There were moments when I thought all the pieces would never fall into place, but they did. In two months I was able to sell the house and make all the arrangements to ship our furniture to Kenya. We had invested everything in the move, but Otieno was confident this was the right decision, and I was almost as excited about our new home as he was. My heart had gone with him and the babies two months before, so the rest of my body just naturally followed.

The first half of our trip was a brief and lovely dream. Our eight-hour layover in Zurich was a breathtaking beginning. After checking into our room, I threw myself onto one of the beds, and my body sunk deeply into the plush down comforter and pillows. Missy threw herself onto her princess sized bed, bounced back up and repeated the process ten or fifteen more times until she wore herself out enough to settle into a soft cozy spot. Later, we wandered through the damp, narrow streets, exploring the little shops filled with delicate treasures that were ticketed with strange sounding prices.

Before flying away, we treated ourselves to hot fudge sundaes. The mounds of rich Swiss vanilla ice cream were accompanied by small silver pitchers of melted Swiss chocolate and a silver bowl of thick whipped cream. This elegant presentation of our favorite desert was served on an aging wooden table, covered with a starched white table cloth and linen napkins.

As we began the final phase of our journey, I tried to capture the images of our life in America that would soon melt into only foggy memories, and I couldn't visualize our new life that was still a blank page. So nightmares of my grieving family and their rage at our marriage plagued my thoughts. Why couldn't my doubting family realize that this unusual marriage could be successful? I closed my eyes and envisioned our reunion in the tropical climate where we'd soon be living. I allowed my imagination to dwell on this fantasy for a few moments, trying to drive out the little fears that kept nipping at my confidence.

As our plane touched down in Nairobi, my enthusiasm began to wane. Unfortunately, Missy's enthusiasm nearly vanished, because her stomach was upset during much of the flight from Switzerland, and she was very pale and weak. She had been such a brave little girl, but she lost most of her braveness before landing. My insides were beginning to sympathize with her. Maybe super rich hot fudge sundaes before a long flight wasn't such a good idea. To add to our discomfort, we had to pass through a maze of red tape and official questioning before we were able to clear customs. Finally we were released.

The last leg of our trip had been difficult, and for just a moment I felt anxious. Then I saw Otieno standing with Otiga beside him and little Nekessa in his arms. How could I have survived without them for two months? The joy of being near them and the realization of how far apart we had been, rushed into my mind all at once. When I reached for my baby Nekessa, she just said, "Mommy" and she kept saying only "Mommy" for days. I would never know the fears that haunted her little mind while we were apart.

Otiga looked very different. All of his soft curly hair was gone, and in its place was a boot camp cut. Little Nekessa had tight African braids and a big black eye that she had received from an unyielding bedpost. Standing next to my little black-eyed Kessy (our nickname for Nekessa) was an anxious looking young girl. This was Susan, the twelve-year-old daughter of his brother. Otieno brought her from Sigulu Island to care for our children until I arrived, and I immediately loved her for that reason alone. He wanted Susan to live with us so she could have a better education than she was getting on the island. She would also master her English more quickly with us.

My first image of Kenya was disheartening. Poverty and dirt was everywhere. As we made our way from the outskirts of Nairobi to Thika, we were completely surrounded by a sea of red dirt, spattered with islands of small tin roofs. These battered metal sheets were the only protection from the glaring sun for the families existing in the one room shacks. There were also tired wooden kiosks, covered only by a worn cloth that barely sheltered the produce and drinks that the owners were hoping to sell. Hundreds of bodies clutching their babies and their vegetables drifted around the dusty kiosks.

As we drove away from the city, the tin roofs were replaced by an occasional house and small groupings of wooden roadside kiosks. It was difficult dividing my attention between my beautiful brown babies sitting next to me and my queasy sweet Melissa, who was less than enthusiastic about a bumpy car ride. Our new home bleakly greeted us through the dusty car windows as we travelled for an hour and a half from Nairobi to Thika. Otieno and Otiga battled for center stage all the way. They both had so much to share.

Our temporary home was the Blue Post Inn. The name was perfect. The hotel was a collection of white block cottages, accented with peacock blue posts and doors. The cottages, restaurant, and spacious bar were arranged around the Chania Falls, like theater seating with the falls as center stage. Between the stark white buildings and the soft roar of the falls, was a lush green garden. Small white tables shaded by crisp red, green and white umbrellas, and tropical trees overflowing with hot pink or lemon yellow flowers added splotches of vibrant color to the garden. Small monkeys chattered with each Other as they played at the very top of the trees. The Blue Post Inn offered itself as an intriguing place to begin our life in Thika.

As we settled into our rooms that afternoon, my thoughts were still racing to the rapid American beat, but this little village knew nothing about that pace. Here everyone moved more slowly. Maybe it was because there was no reason to hurry. I loved that thought, I hated to hurry.

Later that evening, Otieno and I were in our room, encompassed by a mosquito net that fell gently around our bed. Our window was open and screen-less. I watched the guard from our window, as he watched the sleeping inn. The heavy beat of the African music pouring out of the hotel bar, and the hot moist air, sweetly scented by the flowering trees, set the mood for our equally sensuous reunion.

The next morning as our family sat at one of the tables in the garden, we were greeted by the little monkeys chattering in the trees above us. Our breakfast was served on silver trays, with silver teapots, and creamers filled with steaming milk. None of this felt real. The past two months of agonizing separation was over. Now we were beginning a new adventure together in Thika, Kenya.

Otieno had accepted a position with Kenya Canners, a company owned by Del Monte. Since his degree from Ohio State was in Food Science and Nutrition, he was offered a position with the "A" staff, or the top-level supervisory staff, which gave him extra benefits. We were given housing, private schooling for our children, a gardener, and an Askari (guard) who came every night at 6:30 P.M. and left every morning at 6:30 A.M. Being the new man on staff, he had to wait for management housing to open up. Until then, we were to live in the new apartments being rented for "A" staff. Otieno, a very proud and stubborn man, came home raving one afternoon. "We won't live in an apartment! We left an excellent home to come to Africa, and we'll have an excellent home here!" So we gave up their housing, and personally paid to rent a house located next to the golf course of the Thika Country Club.

The little town of Thika was located about 40 miles north of Nairobi. It had been one of the villages of the Kikuyu tribe, but the Del Monte pineapple plantation, and a British tanning company, had added money and a little British accent to the area. When Del Monte moved into this fertile farmland, already dotted with coffee plantations, it added miles and miles of immaculately groomed pineapple fields, cared for by a large portion of the town. Located in the center of this huge pineapple plantation was Imani, Del Monte's private British school. Melissa and Otiga would attend school here, along with 200 other children from the Del Monte staff and the surrounding area.

Melissa was understandably nervous about the first day of school, and she returned that evening even more concerned. The British school system placed each child in a seat according to how well he was doing academically. The first seat in the front row was given to the student with the highest average, and so on. She was worried about where she would be placed. There were two other Americans in her third grade class who helped her get over this fear. She eventually took to Imani like a fish to water, possibly because she spent so much time in the water.

She had a two hour lunch break each day. The students would hurry through lunch and then spend the rest of the time swimming. Her nose was always burned and her hair was usually green from the chlorine.

Otiga was in the pre-kindergarten class, and he immediately fit in. He would come home each day with wonderful tales of all the monsters his team had captured. Very little was shared about all the letters of the alphabet he had mastered or his coloring skills, but I was pleased that he was preparing himself for an exciting career in monster slaying.

Our typical day would start at 6:30 A.M. as the sun began showing off its brilliance. John, our semi-sleeping askari, would slowly wander off our compound to join the other askaris, who were also finishing their nightly duties at the various homes in our neighborhood. This particular morning was different. The askaris all remained to discuss the previous night's activities. The Japanese Ambassador, who lived about ten houses down from us, had been robbed and then stabbed as he attempted to defend his home from the thieves. When we first arrived in Thika, I was shocked by the large cement walls with permanently embedded broken glass that surrounded many houses. The locked gates, the bars on all the doors and windows, the askaris, and the guard dogs had astonished me. However, after being awakened in the middle of the night by piercing sirens and deep foghorns, I understood. This chorus of soprano and baritone sirens was Thika's neighborhood watch. Because the local police were not concerned with break-ins, it was up to each neighborhood to handle the problems.

Unfortunately, this night the thieves were well prepared, because the guard of the family had orchestrated the robbery. Since the Ambassador's family was planning to return to Japan in a day or so, all of their belongings were packed. This was very convenient for the thieves because everything was ready to transport in a hurry. The robbers were not captured, the man was seriously injured, and the family lost most of their possessions. This experience left a vivid impression in my mind, and John, our askari, finished painting the final frightening brush strokes on this picture for me. That morning he announced, "I can no longer be your askari. This street has too many robberies. I have a family, and I can't risk my life being a guard here."

Otieno's work schedule required him to supervise two weeks on day shift, then two weeks on night shift. And of course, he was on the night shift now! I had no phone, no siren, no dog – and now, no askari. I did have three small children, and a twelve-year-old girl who spoke only a little English. I was frightened, but I didn't know anyone to call even if I had a phone, which I didn't have. I was told that I wouldn't have a phone for many months because nothing was done quickly here. God was very real during those nights, and my trust in Him grew. It was also a blessing that the days were very difficult, because by night I was so tired I could sleep in spite of the possible dangers.

The days were more challenging because none of our possessions had arrived yet, and they would not arrive for months. Some of Otieno's co-workers had volunteered to share the necessities, so we were able to begin "playing house." We had mattresses on the floor, a couch, two chairs, a few cooking pots and some dishes. We used a sheet in the middle of the dining room floor for our daily picnic style meals. We had a stove that didn't work, and no refrigerator. I learned how to cook meals on an African charcoal grill. By putting a skillet on the grill and covering it with a tin pie plate, I had a small oven. I could even bake biscuits and cookies.

I had no washer or dryer, but we had lots of laundry, so I used the bathtub. Washing the clothes wasn't too difficult, but ringing them out was tough, especially the blue jeans and towels. Susan was an incredible help with this, and the hours we spent together was a special time of bonding. We learned from each other as we tackled the many challenges each of us was facing in our new home. After we manually squeezed out the water, Melissa and the little ones helped lay the wet clothes all over the grassy hill behind our house. This worked pretty well until the rainy season came. Rain made everything more difficult in Thika, but it was so important.

It didn't take me long to discover that life in Kenya differed from life in the United States in just about everyway. We didn't have a car yet, so one afternoon, Otieno took me out in a friend's car for a driving lesson. Driving on the left side of the road was an interesting difference. It wasn't terribly awkward, but it took some concentration.

The most important part of driving was watching out for the numerous pedestrians who were walking along the side of the road. The majority of the people didn't have cars. Often the women would have small children hopping and skipping beside them. I was astonished at how fast most people drove on the narrow, winding, unlit two-way roads, and at the number of pedestrians who were killed, especially at night. Speed limit signs were ignored and speeding tickets just weren't done, so many pedestrians were put at risk by these speed demons.

No matter how dangerous it was to ride in a car on the narrow roads, it was nothing compared to a matatu ride. These old, battered mini-buses were the main transportation for many Kenyans. One hot afternoon we needed to go to Nairobi, so Otieno and I walked into Thika to catch the matatu. "Catching it" was the perfect description for what we had to do, because there were many more people than there were seats. He asked the driver if we could ride in the front, because only three people were permitted to sit there, but there was no limit in the back. If you could squeeze in, you could ride. He allowed me to sit in the front, but not Otieno.

Every seat was overflowing on the matatu before we began the trip, and even as we moved, people were jumping onto the van. Some of the men just held on to the open window and stood outside on the running board. By the time we were actually on the road to Nairobi, the mini-bus felt more like a sardine can than a vehicle, with extra sardines hanging out on all sides. Matatus and buses had no air conditioning, and since it was a very hot day the closeness made the heat even hotter, and the sweat ever sweatier. Many of the women had bags of produce under their legs, and a child or two in their laps. Some of the passengers took this opportunity to eat their lunches, while others puffed on cigarettes, adding to the aroma of this bouquet of life.

I was doing fine until the man sitting very close to me decided to put his hand up my dress. I was so shocked that I screamed, and pulled his hand off me as I tried to move farther away from him. There wasn't an inch of extra space, but the driver must have witnessed what had happened, because he immediately banished the man to the back of the van, and allowed Otieno to move to the front. I sat very quietly for the remainder of the trip; grateful that the driver was such a sympathetic gentleman.

It had been less than a month since we had arrived, and already the red soil of Thika was in my blood, and my heart had begun to beat with a slower pace. I loved awakening to the sounds that floated through our open, screen-less window. Our alarm clock was the neighbor's rooster, and our morning music was a live concert performed by a quartet of multicolored birds. Actually, a real alarm clock would have been nice, but our shipment hadn't arrived yet. Several mornings a week I would walk to town to buy groceries. This was one of my favorite chores. With Kessy wrapped snugly on my back and the locally woven basket over my shoulder, we would begin our walk up the hill from our house. We would always go very early, before the sun's heat took control of the day.

I would wear my usual Thika uniform, a long sundress and sandals. Since I was married to a native, I had to abide by the local dress standards while I was in town. Shorts were unacceptable attire for women, and considered vulgar by many of the natives. Pants or slacks were the trademark of the local prostitutes. If I was going to "fit in" I had to avoid these clothes. The long sundress met with Otieno's approval, and it was comfortable for me.

I never felt afraid as I walked to town, even though some of the British women felt that it was not safe to walk anywhere without a man. This was such a peaceful time for me. I loved passing by the giant banana plants that were dripping with tiny finger bananas and the multi-colored trees drenched in vibrant red and lemon yellow flowers. My favorite was the Jacaranda tree that dropped delicate purple petals, so that the red dirt path took on the appearance of being covered with pale purple snow.

We would usually stop at The Blue Post Inn, which was about half way. I would order Cokes for Kessy and me, and then we'd chat with the waiters, who had become friends with the children during the two months they lived there before my arrival. We would then walk down to the Chania Falls to watch the water pour over the rocks and wind lazily towards town. After a few moments of lingering here, we would also head leisurely into town.

I felt so accepted by the local residents as they smiled or waved at us as we walked up the hill to Thika. They were accustomed to seeing white people in town, but they always drove in, got their supplies, and drove away, seldom lingering, and never walking with a brown baby secured on their backs.

It was the custom here for the native women to be addressed as the mother of their eldest son, and since Otiga was my only son, I became known as "Mama Otiga".

There were only three white women married to native men in Thika. All three of the women were from America, and all the men were from the Luhya tribe and worked at Del Monte. We were somewhat of a novelty. This could have added extra pressure to our life, but everyone in this community was so kind to us that we felt like we belonged.

Shopping in town was a new experience to be treasured. Small dukas (shops) and large bars colorfully lined the town from one end to the other. Also running down the entire length of the town, just below the sidewalk, was a narrow open gutter. This was the town's sewer system. Pouring out of the bars and into the street was not only the dirty water but also the heavy beat of the local music, which worked like a mythical siren, luring in the patrons. The bars were never empty, and the shops were never full; of food, that is. There was always a shortage of something!

Sitting in front of the shops were men offering various services. Either in a broken form of English, or in Swahili, they would advertise their skills.

"Need a nice dress? I can make it for you," came from the man sitting behind an old pump sewing machine.

Haircut, four shillings," offered a man sitting on a stool, holding a pair of scissors.

"New rubber on the soles of your shoes makes them like new," promised another tradesman from his sidewalk location.

Shopping was simple. There were very few decisions to be made in selecting the groceries. As I entered the duka, I would greet the storekeeper behind the counter, "Jambo" (Swahili for "hello").

"Mzuri sana, Mama Otiga," he answered with a big smile. "What do you need today?" He offered a hard candy to Kessy. I untied my kanga (a large piece of brightly colored material worn by the women to wrap their babies securely on their backs as they walked or did chores) and gently dropped Kessy off my back. She took the "sweet," and then wandered around the little shop while I gave my grocery list to the shopkeeper.

"I need two loaves of bread, a box of Omo, ten eggs, a jar of peanut butter, and three packets of milk, please," I told him. I gave him my cardboard egg holder, and my woven bag. Egg cartons and grocery bags weren't furnished, so I had to supply them or do without. It didn't take long to fill my order. There weren't choices of which brand of detergent or peanut butter. There was bread, not different types like rye, butter crust, or stone ground wheat. There was "peanut butter," not Jiffy or Skippy, not smooth or crunchy. Omo was the only choice of detergent.

There were a few American brands on the shelves, but they were too expensive to buy. A small can of tuna was $2.50, and a box of tampons was $10.00. Items like spaghetti, boxed cereal, and crackers were economically out of the question. Cheese, brown sugar, flour, and rice were often unavailable. The milk was packaged in small waxed paper packets, and was kept un-refrigerated in metal tubs on the floor of the shop. It was probably wise to buy milk early in the morning, before it became too warm. There was no ice to keep anything cold. There wasn't even ice for the drinks that were served in the bars or restaurants.

All of this was relatively unimportant to the local people, because their daily diet often consisted of ugali and sukumi-weeki. Ugali is corn meal or ground cassava, where it is grown. It is boiled in water to make a thick pasty substance. Sukumi-weeki is the African version of boiled greens. The ugali is dipped into the sukumi-weeki broth and eaten.

One evening, after walking home from town with the groceries, washing the clothes by hand in the bath tub, and cooking our evening meal on the jiko, I served dinner on a sheet on the dining room floor. We had sukumi-weeki and Ugali like most of the families in Thika. Melissa was adjusting quite well to her new environment, but she was tired of eating boiled greens again. She longed for a good old American hamburger. However, the following evening, Otieno brought home a rare treat and local delicacy, flying termites. Our new askari, also from the Luhya tribe, had caught a ten-gallon bucket of these winged creatures, and he was excited about sharing them with us. OT taught me how to fry them so that they were crisp and crunchy. Otiga, Nekessa, Susan, and Otieno munched on this tasty treat for days. However, after Melissa tasted the fried termites, she decided that boiled greens and corn meal wasn't that bad after all. Fortunately this delicacy was only available when the termites swarmed out of the ground, which was a seasonal occurrence.

# CHAPTER 3: SIGULU ISLAND

## *So Much Sand, So Little Joy*

It was early in December and I had been in Kenya for only a few months. I had adjusted well to our new life, but now it was time for the real test of my flexibility. I had shared Otieno's island life vicariously for more than four years. It was time to take the final step into his world. Excitement and anxiety battled for control of my thoughts. I wanted to see where he had played, hear the sounds, and smell the fragrances that filled his senses as he was growing into the man I loved. I was a little leery about tasting the food, but three out of four wasn't bad.

But what if his family refused to accept me, just as mine had refused to accept him? Would we have to go through that pain again? No one on Sigulu Island had ever married a white woman, and many of the small children had never seen a white person.

The journey from Thika to the island involved an eight-hour bus ride, a two-hour jeep ride through the bush to Port Victoria, on the coast of Kenya, and a thirty minute canoe ride to the island. Sigulu Island is in Lake Victoria. We left the children with friends because we would be gone for many days and we felt the trip would be too difficult for them. Actually, I had no idea how difficult, and unforgettable, this pilgrimage was going to be.

Buses in Kenya can best be described by comparing them to 1960 vintage school buses with no shock absorbers. They were made to carry 45 children and their books, but here they actually carried 50 to 60 adults, with their boxes, bags, chickens, and produce. Air conditioning is not an option for most places in Kenya; possibly in the expensive hotels in large cities, but not in the homes, schools, or shops, and definitely not on the buses. Comfort is a concept that is ignored because it just isn't available.

As I sat next to Otieno and observed the passengers, it was like seeing a filled canvass overflowing with life. Each person on this over-packed bus had a story accompanying him. I enjoyed watching all the activity and I noticed that since I was the only white person on the bus, they seemed to enjoy watching me also.

My companions had no idea there were comfortable means of transportation available in other parts of the world. As we bumped and jerked along, with the chickens squawking, the children chattering, and the boxes and bags bulging out into the small aisle, our bus suddenly came to a screeching halt. Before I could whisper a "why" to Otieno, two local police officers entered the bus and began walking down the small aisle, scanning the passengers and their belongings. I watched them intently as they silently scrutinized each person. When they reached my seat, they stopped and their eyes settled on me, as did every other eye on the bus. I sat perfectly still with my eyes looking down, as I had learned to do with all African men, hoping they would move on. They didn't.

"What do you have," one of them barked at me, as both of them came in closer for the kill. I felt like a wounded animal being circled by vultures. Why had they stopped the bus? Why were they questioning me? My voice quivered as I pushed my words out as strongly as I could, "All I have is this." I offered them my suitcase as I spoke.

They looked quickly at the luggage and said, "Open it." Their faces were stern as they watched me fumble with my bag. They rooted through my things without comment, then as quickly as they had appeared, they disappeared from the bus. They didn't speak to or search anyone else.

Otieno whispered to me in a less than convincing voice, "Don't worry, dear. The police often stop cars and buses to search them. They probably searched you because it's unusual for a white person to be traveling this way." I was still feeling a little uneasy when the bus stopped again about an hour later.

"Why are we stopping now?" I murmured, as I looked down the isle for more uniforms. I didn't see any police, but I did notice a number of people leaving the bus.

"This is a bathroom break," he casually answered. I looked around. We were in the middle of nowhere, and yet many people were still getting off the bus. Since I also needed to make this side trip, I looked outside to see where everyone was headed. There was nothing outside, not even bushes or trees. The passengers were just squatting on the road beside the bus. I had used the public bathrooms with only a hole in the floor that required strategic squatting. I was even prepared to go behind a bush when we arrived on the island, because there were no bathrooms, but at this moment I just couldn't squat on the road in front of everyone. "I'll try to make it a little longer."

The pressure in my kidneys added to the uncomfortable ride, and the bumpy ride added to the pressure on my kidneys. Some time later we had another "pit stop" without the pit. I still couldn't join the others on the road, even though it was becoming a nagging necessity. By the third stop, the pain was more demanding than my anxiety. It was a good time to venture out because now it was dark, and there were some bushes just a short distance away. Otieno walked with me into the darkness. The trip was much more enjoyable now, as we bumped along to our destination. We rode all night and into the morning.

As the sun began depositing its warmth onto the soil, the bus deposited us on a small dirt road in Busia, a neighboring village of Port Victoria, which was our destination. We had successfully survived the bus ride. Now Otieno's task was to find a jeep and a driver to take us through the bush. From Port Victoria we would take a canoe to the island.

Sitting on my bag by the side of the dusty road gave me ample time to think. This trip was the beginning of an even greater understanding of God's faithfulness and His daily care. The fire of this African heat was molding and shaping a new me, one that would never again doubt the reality of God's presence in my life. It was good I was learning this lesson now, because I would need His strength and comfort in the days and months to come.

The jeep did come, and Otieno arranged with the driver to take us over the pothole ridden dirt paths into Port Victoria. It was now time to take a canoe trip into his world, and to meet my new family.

The canoe ride across Lake Victoria was slow and soothing. When we reached the island, we stepped out of reality and into a Humphrey Bogart movie. The land gently met the water, and then dramatically pulled away into a steep jungle-covered hill. Our boat cut smoothly into the endless white sandy beach. My heart raced with the anticipation of meeting his family.

A small group of men helped us unload our bags. They all seemed to be grinning at me as they spoke with Otieno. He had insisted that I wear a long-sleeved, cotton suede dress – with heels! Why I listened to him was unclear to me at this moment. I decided that if I survived this trip, I would never listen to him about clothes again. As we walked up the steep hill, through the thick bush and sandy soil, I fell behind the others. When we eventually reached a clearing, I saw my first village hut. It was a round structure made of reddish brown mud, with a roof made from piles of large leaves. It had an arched opening for the door, with no covering over it. As Otieno talked with the men around this hut, I could see the joy on his face. He was not just happy to be home; he was excited that I was with him.

Everyone seemed to be talking at once - everyone but me, that is. I wasn't saying anything, but I knew my presence was felt. As we moved up the hill our procession grew larger. Each little hut we passed released more people into our group.

Everyone was happy except the children! They hid behind their mothers, and screamed or cried. Otieno laughed and explained, "They have never seen anyone like you, Carole. They think you are a wild animal because of the blonde hair around your face. Your hair looks like a mane to them." We were definitely creating quite a stir in this little hidden village. As we approached our destination the intensity of the voices reached a peak. I knew we were home.

Sitting outside a hut was a very small, very black, very old woman. She was barefoot, with a kanga wrapped around her frail body, and a faded cloth tied around her thin gray hair. Her eyes were scarcely open, and her movements were labored. She put down a small hand-made clay pipe, and carefully rose from the mat. She slowly moved toward Otieno, and he raced to her. I knew this was Auma, his mother. I loved her immediately. Her eyes were sore and tired, but at this moment they glistened with the radiance of a mother's love. I could see many of Otieno's features in this blessed woman who was now holding both of his hands. The eight-hour bus ride with no bathrooms, and the long sweaty trek up the sandy overgrown hill, was now worth it. A tear fell from her cloudy, half-blind eyes. I understood her joy.

We were taken to a hut just down the hill from his mother's hut. All the older children who weren't afraid of me walked with us, and the younger children cautiously followed behind. At each clearing, women sat on mats beating and grinding the thick wood-like stems of a strange looking broad-leafed plant. Otieno explained to me that this was the cassava plant, a staple of their diet. Small, naked toddlers with large tummies played in the dirt near the women.

We reached the hut that was to be our shelter while we were here. Otieno was aglow with this moment; it was something he had dreamed about for years. I was aglow also, but it was with fever. Unfortunately, diarrhea and nausea accompanied the fever. Otieno suggested I rest while he visited with his family. "Why don't you bring your mother here so you can visit alone with her for awhile," I offered. The brightness of his eyes dimmed, and his entire face frowned as he spoke with a reprimand in his voice, "My mother is never allowed in my hut, and she can never be on my cot! This is totally against our beliefs." He wasn't angry with me, just amazed that I didn't understand.

Before he left the hut, his voice became stern. "Don't allow anyone to take anything off of you or cut your hair. It could be used for black magic against you. I'm afraid my brother, Pascal, will do this." With that comforting thought, he left.

I began looking around our brown mud room, with its matching dirt floor. There were no luxuries or frills, just a single cot against one wall. There were no windows, electricity, or water. I knew this before we arrived, but standing here, made the reality of their daily lives so bleak. I wasn't able to dwell very long on this thought, because my stomach was revolting. I was prepared to use the great outdoors, but I hadn't expected to be sick, nor had I imagined an audience of children accompanying me everywhere. This was what I found when I walked outside. To the children, I was new and different, like a new toy. They had not yet tired of me, so they followed me. The final humbling experience was using Mother Nature's toilet paper. I just hoped the leaves I chose were not harmful. The children had given me some space and time, so when I felt a little better, I awkwardly fumbled my way through the bush and returned to my hut.

The privacy was such a relief. I changed my clothes because the heels and suede dress were hot, uncomfortable, and totally stupid for a mud hut. I had just finished dressing when three women burst through the opening. They were laughing and speaking in Abaluhya, the native language of the Luhya tribe. They kept pointing to the sundress I had just put on, and then pointing to themselves. Finally, one woman pulled lightly on the dress. She wanted it; so I gave it to her. They left the hut very excited. It was better for her to have the dress. I had other sundresses with me, and I doubted that she did.

I was still feeling weak and I needed to rest. The only furniture in the hut was the narrow cot against the wall. I thought if I could lie down my stomach would settle down; so I went to the cot. Allowing my mind to wander, I noticed an intricate pattern in the mud wall next to me. I pulled myself onto the wooden rim of the cot to examine the wall more closely. Spiders! The intricate design was actually hundreds of spiders building their homes in the mud. The wall was literally crawling with spiders. The sudden burst of adrenaline from this discovery filled me with enough energy that I no longer needed to rest. It was time to join my newfound family.

I found my way back to Auma's hut and joined the women who were sitting on mats outside of her hut. I watched them as they talked. Auma was dressed in the traditional kanga; a long piece of bright material wrapped around the waist and tucked in. She spoke no English and I spoke only limited Abaluhya so we were unable to communicate with words, but as I sat next to her I felt her approval. I had learned much about Auma through Otieno, and I had caught a love for his mother from him. I didn't know how old she was, but neither did she. Her tired eyes were clouded over with cataracts and they were swollen, possibly from the red dirt that constantly filled the air. Her feet were also swollen and covered with sores. She didn't wear shoes. I wondered if she didn't wear shoes because her feet were sore, or if she didn't have any shoes to wear. It had been difficult for me to imagine the lifestyle of his mother when Otieno had described it to me. Now, actually seeing her, made the reality of her existence much too painful. She had lived all of her life on this island and she knew nothing else.

Auma was the second of five wives owned by Habembe, Otieno's father. He had been the chief of the village. She had her own hut, as did the other four wives. Her children had slept in the hut until they reached puberty, the magic age that meant they could no longer remain with her. I wondered, as I watched Auma move, if she was as ancient as she appeared, or if she had simply grown old before her time because her life had been so demanding and uninspiring.

Auma, now a widow, had given birth to nearly a dozen babies, but she had only three children left to care for her in her old age. A crocodile had eaten one son while he was bathing in the lake. Another grown son had died suddenly with no visible cause. The babies had died easily and often. I knew Otieno was one of the highlights of her life, because sons were the only children that counted. He was her baby boy, who had returned to her as a conqueror from far off lands.

What did Auma look forward to? Her life was filled with uninspiring sameness. Each day she would rise from her thin foam mat that was lying on the dirt floor of her hut. She would join the other women at the lake to bathe, wash clothes, and then fill buckets with the same dirty water for the day's cooking and drinking. She would eat the same food day after day, sukumi-weeki and ugali. Occasionally she would supplement this with some boiled fish or an egg. She had never eaten chicken; that was always saved for the men. She was a good woman; she knew her place and she didn't stray from it. There was no joy in her tired old eyes, but as I surveyed the other women, I saw none in theirs either.

Most of the women were grinding the cassava root as they sat and talked. One woman, tall and muscular, was standing alone at the side of the hut. She was stooped over three rocks that were encompassing the fire. I watched her as she worked without stopping. The outdoors was her kitchen and the three rocks surrounding the fire was her stove. She also looked tired and old beyond her years. Otieno had told me about this woman. She was Akinyi, the wife of his older brother, Otiga, and the mother of Susan, the twelve-year-old girl who was living with us. When Otiga had died suddenly, according to custom, Otieno, the closest brother, inherited Akinyi. The two small, frail children by her side were Peter and Juliet. He and Akinyi were their parents.

Peter was around nine years old, and Juliet was probably eight, but they looked seven and six. Otieno had been responsible for Akinyi and the children until she remarried. He told me that she had married while he was in America. I watched Peter and Juliet as they played. They didn't smile or show any affection for Akinyi, nor did she for them. It seemed as though they were void of any happy emotions. I was saddened by the severity of their lives. These beautiful little ones knew nothing of playgrounds with swings and slides. There were no bicycles, building blocks, or toy trucks anywhere. Even the endless stretch of sand and the cool waves of Lake Victoria were used primarily as a tool for survival; not as a source of pleasure because of the never-ending fear of crocodiles. But somehow, these resourceful children managed to create fun out of nothing. Old rags magically turned into a soccer ball, sticks were transformed into swords, and wire from somewhere was twisted and bent into the form of a car. As long as they were safe and not hungry, they would find a way to play.

One of the reasons we had come to the island was to take Peter and Juliet home with us. I wondered how Akinyi felt about this. I hurt for her, when I thought how empty I had felt without my children when they left for Africa with Otieno. I wanted to tell her I would take good care of them, but she wouldn't understand me. Instead I prayed, "Please, God, give her a peace about this. Help her to feel your comfort and help me to show the children your love." There were no opportunities on this island, and we could make a difference in their lives. This was the only way to give them an education, and to help Akinyi with their care. The language barrier would be challenging, but we were excited about doing this. I hoped Akinyi wanted it also.

Akinyi had been preparing a meal for everyone. She had done this with only the two large pots that were cooking over three massive stones. I admired and respected her. This lifestyle was all she had ever known. Day after day she walked miles carrying heavy pots to the lake to get water. Week after week she returned to the lake to wash clothes and bathe children. No wonder she never smiled. Each day must have seemed like the last one... the last one... the last one...

The only difference in her routine was the weather. Now it was December, the hot, dry season. I tried to imagine the village during the big rains. Red mud everywhere! At least now everyone could be outside together. I wondered how they managed being held captive in the huts for days by the rains. Maybe the changaa, (moonshine) they drank, helped to deaden their senses and make reality a little less real. The lifeless, blank stares of some of the women supported this theory.

It was time for the meal. A large bowl of ugali was taken to the men first. I was taken into Auma's hut, where the food had been placed on a mat in the center of the floor. A child brought a bowl of water for me to wash my hands, and then left without ever allowing her eyes to meet mine. I was alone. All the women were just outside the hut, eating and talking. I hoped it wasn't something I had said – or rather hadn't said, since I really couldn't say much in their language.

When I looked inside one of the bowls a fish head stared back at me. Another new experience. It had been a day full of new experiences. It would have been easier to face this fish if my stomach hadn't been so unsettled. I thought to myself, "I must learn to like this!" Otieno had been raised on boiled fish in a soup, and ugali. He had been more fortunate than the Kenyans who lived inland. Many of them didn't have fish regularly. I had become accustomed to corn meal ugali, but cassava ugali was like eating ground glass held together by paste. I did the best I could with the meal, and hoped the small amount I had eaten would not offend anyone. When I left the hut, the children came in and finished the food I hadn't eaten, so I felt better about it.

I returned to my mat outside of Auma's hut just in time to see the men returning from their meal. They were like over-grown boys, laughing and talking. Otieno was enjoying every moment of being home. The faces of the men seemed to reflect more life than did the women's faces. They didn't look as tired or burdened. As the men paraded past us, a slightly taller, older man came into view. It seemed rather odd to me that he was wearing a long-sleeved shirt, long pants, and high rubber boots in this heat.

When he grinned, his missing front teeth caused his smile to appear evil. Then I looked into his eyes and the ugly black depths of his soul poured out. This was an evil man! This had to be Otieno's older brother, Pascal. Now I understood his concern about witchcraft. I turned my face away from him, but I knew he was still grinning his evil grin. It was his village, he was the chief and he was in charge! Otieno sat down beside me and whispered, "Pascal just ordered a goat to be slaughtered in your honor. He has never killed a goat in anyone's honor before!" This was truly a sign of my acceptance. I should have been pleased, but I wasn't. As Pascal talked to me through Otieno's interpretation, I understood why.

"You know woman, if anything should happen to Habembe, I would get you as my wife," he said through his horrid grin. I knew I would have no say in this matter because I was a woman. If anything happened to Otieno while we were here, I would become a prisoner on this little island because no one would go against Pascal, and none of my family had any idea where this village was located. Otieno's strained voice told me he was also uncomfortable with Pascal's questions and comments. As more and more people joined the celebration, Pascal left the inner circle and went with the men who were skinning the goat. He returned shortly and sat down on the ground in front of me. Speaking through Otieno, he put a ring of goatskin in my hand. I turned to my husband for his translation, but he told me nothing as he grabbed the skin from my hand and returned it to Pascal.

"This could be used as black magic against you! Don't ever allow that ring to be put on your finger, and don't let anyone take anything off of you," he whispered as he glared at his brother. My mind re-wound to earlier that day when the women had come into my hut.

Staring at the red dirt, I muttered, "I already have. Three women came into the hut wanting my sundress, so I gave it to them. They were so happy about getting it; I didn't think it was a problem."

"Carole, you don't understand do you? This man has powers that are strong and evil." His eyes began scanning the women. "Which woman took the dress?" My eyes joined his as we looked for her.

"There, in the back, standing off by herself. She has a red cloth around her head," I said as I pointed with my glance.

"That's Pascal's number-one wife." Otieno whispered as he lowered his head into his hands. I closed my eyes and breathed in slowly, allowing myself time to digest this information. Pascal was an evil man, and he had made it clear that this was his village and if anything should happen to Otieno, I would remain here as one of his wives. I could not dwell on this vile thought. Fear was one of the tools Pascal used to control the island. Then, I remembered the antidote to my fear. Pascal had evil within him, but I had the Holy Spirit within me! I didn't need to be afraid. I thanked God for this truth and asked Him to bind Satan from us, to protect us from evil. I prayed that I could show my new family the Love of Jesus through my actions, because I couldn't tell them with my words.

The goat Pascal had killed for me was completely skinned now. Some of the meat was roasted, and some was put in a pot for boiling. The blood was also poured into a pot and cooked over the stones. The long elastic intestines were cut open and laid on the ground to dry. Nothing was wasted.

Otieno, aware of my fever and my internal turmoil, sent one of the children somewhere to get a Coke for me. I enjoyed the thought of this village with no toilets, no electricity, and not even toilet paper having Coke! It made me realize the marketing power of the Coca-Cola Company! I was very thankful for it at this moment. Even warm, it settled my stomach.

The day was almost over. Otieno and I walked to the lake as the sun was slowly setting. The magnificent shades of reds and oranges swirled into warm colorful patterns just above the water. We were alone now. We undressed and he held me in his arms as the waves rocked us gently. The cool water felt soothing against my feverish body. As if the heat of the sun was so intense that it could wait no longer, it plunged into the lake and melted.

It was dark now, and everyone was huddled inside one of the huts. Changaa flowed freely, as did the small cubes of tobacco-like changaa. There was a huge hurricane lamp focusing its attention on Pascal's face, and highlighting the endless evil in his eyes. He was in the center of the hut, shouting in a piercing agitated voice. His tone continued to rise in volume until it seemed to fill the hut and explode in my ears. Pascal was violently angry, as he sliced the air with his hands to reinforce his rage. As he barked out words, he would occasionally direct his horrid grin at me. Otieno didn't translate what Pascal was saying. He took hold of my hand and said, "Carole, I don't think you should stay here any longer." He led me out of the hut amid the screams gushing from Pascal's mouth.

It felt good to be outside in the cool night air. As we walked down the hill to our hut, Otieno whispered, "You must stay here, and I must go back and face Pascal." That meant I must face the hut, the spiders, and the night alone! Not a comforting thought. I knew however, I had the easier task. By this time I was truly exhausted. I realized that I couldn't stay awake all night and watch the spiders, so I passionately asked God to please watch over me.

Sometime during the night, Otieno joined me on our little cot. He didn't share the events of the evening. I knew if he wanted to tell me about the conflict with Pascal, he would, and if he didn't, no questioning could pull it from him. I could only imagine; and then I decided that imagining wasn't a good idea. I needed to drive Pascal from my mind. We slept like nesting spoons on the small cot beneath the netting that protected us from the malaria-carrying mosquitoes. I doubted that the net would keep away the spiders. With Otieno next to me, I was pushed even closer to the wall. I eased myself more tightly into him, attempting to move as far from the wall of spiders as possible. Otieno thought I was asking for him, and his body immediately answered yes. I slept the rest of the night safely blanketed by my husband.

I didn't see Pascal that morning nor any other time before we left. I thought about the conflict in the hut, and wondered how it ended. I was thankful I didn't have to avoid Pascal's eyes this morning.

It was almost time to leave the island. As we began our long walk down to the other side of the beach, many of my new relatives and friends came to say good-bye. An aunt brought a live duck as a going-away present. A very old woman gave me three eggs, and a young pregnant girl handed me two dried fish, carefully wrapped in paper. I knew what special gifts these were, and my heart was deeply touched.

While we waited for the canoe, Peter and Juliet appeared, carrying a small ragged cloth bag tied together with rope. Akinyi wasn't with the children. Was she too upset to see them off? I wondered if she had any say in this decision, or if Otieno had decided without asking her. I wished I could reassure her, but I never saw Akinyi again.

We began our journey home with two frightened children and Sabah, our first ayah, all of whom spoke only Abaluhya. The bus was, of course, grossly overloaded and under-repaired. I had my duck, three eggs, and the dried fish to protect. My heart was bursting from the love and kindness my new family had shown me. I didn't see the three women who took my sundress, nor Pascal, before we left, and Otieno didn't mention them again. I was glad I had so many experiences to play back in my mind; it would make the long uncomfortable trip shorter. As we rode along, and the shock-less bus rocked us not so gently in our broken seats, an old Latin saying popped into my mind. "We came, we saw, we conquered." I thought about this saying and our trip. "We came, we saw, we were accepted and loved." This was a much better ending.

# CHAPTER 4: THE HABEMBE GROUP

## *So Many Children*

Time passed quickly after we returned home with our new additions to the family. Peter and Juliet added a whole new dimension to our already diverse family, as well as a few new challenges. The first day we arrived home, Otieno was showing the children around the house, explaining each room. After the guided tour, Peter went into the bathroom. Soon after he came out, Melissa went in, only to return immediately. "Mom, someone wet all over the floor," she whispered. He had explained to Peter that this room was where he was to "go," but not how to do it, so Peter just urinated on the floor. He had no idea how to use the toilet because he had never seen one before.

Peter's heart and my heart immediately bonded together. He seemed to thrive on hugs and homemade cookies, and I never tired of supplying them. We had a working stove and a refrigerator now, so I baked often for the children. That is until the flour ran out and there was none available anywhere.

Juliet was somewhat slower in responding to her new life. She was like a frightened little kitten taken from its mother. Her small eyes exposed her loneliness. She withdrew from any type of affection. I ached for Juliet, knowing she missed her real mother and all that was familiar and safe to her. I hoped that in time she would adjust to this new life. With six playful children in the house, it would be difficult for her to stay distant for very long. Besides, Christmas was almost here, and I had so much to teach them about this magnificent day, the birthday of our Lord, Jesus Christ, and why this day is so important.

Today was December 24th. This was not going to be the typical Christmas I had grown to love in America. Our furniture had not yet arrived, so we were still camping out. I excused myself from this reality, as I trudged up the hill towards town. The sounds, sights and smells of Christmas in America surrounded me as I took a brief trip into the past. Christmas is carols, telling the story of the birth of Jesus. Christmas programs and presents celebrating His birthday. Christmas is pine needles and cold crisp nights, all lit up with twinkling lights.

All the trimmings of Christmas I had known were missing here. There would be no snow. The streets and stores were not decorated with tinsel and holly, or anything else. There were no wreaths, or trees with ornaments. No Christmas carols flowed from the stores. Life went on as usual for everyone in this little village. The Christmas fever that over-took America for well over a month before the big day had not infected this slow-paced community.

I came back into reality as The Blue Post Inn came into sight. The sun had been awake for an hour. It was 7:30 A.M. and still pleasantly cool as I continued the dusty trip with Kessy wrapped on my back. This three-mile walk was a peaceful time to be alone with my thoughts. I loved to feel the warm red soil brush past my sandals and lightly cover my toes. The sun's intensity was not yet demanding my attention, so I could enjoy the gentle warmth against my face.

I stopped for coffee at the Blue Post. I rarely hurried anywhere; it just wasn't done. Kessy and I sat at one of the umbrella-covered tables in the garden. I loved watching the "well-bred tourists" from all over the world. They strolled under the flowering trees, stopping to watch the native artists carve African figures out of wood. I felt sorry for them. They were able to spend only brief moments absorbing the beauty around them, but I could return day after day for refills.

David, one of the waiters, brought me back into focus, "Coffee, Mama Otiga?" I accepted his offer and ordered Kessy a Coke and chips (the British name for French fries). As we rested, my thoughts drifted over the past weeks of pre-Christmas preparations.

Having lived in America, Otieno was aware of the adjustment I was facing, so he tried to help. "Carole, Terri told me about a Women's League garage sale. She will pick you up if you'd like to look for Christmas presents." This was a brilliant idea because I was having trouble finding gifts for our six children. Then he smiled a confident grin as his voice purred, "And I'll have flour for you sometime this week."

There had been no flour for over a month! I could cope with no Christmas tree, no Christmas music in the stores, and second-hand presents, but I couldn't imagine Christmas without Christmas cookies and our traditional cinnamon bread. He had made my day, and his face glowed with pride.

"How can you get flour?" I asked with the excitement of a child. "I've tried everywhere – there isn't any!"

He made the most of this moment of glory as he revealed his secret source. "The Vice President in charge of production has extra flour that his wife brought back from England. He's giving us two packets." A packet was a five-pound bag of flour. I was ecstatic! As he promised, he returned home that evening with two packets of flour, presenting them to me like a knight presenting a slaughtered dragon.

All week I guarded the treasured flour. Meanwhile, the children and I made paper Christmas decorations to adorn the house for this special occasion. With each paper ring we pasted to the next one, we sang Christmas Carols. Peter, and Juliet had no idea what we were singing about, but they seemed more than willing to listen intently as they pasted. Our hearts were communicating, even though our words were not.

The children caught the Christmas excitement, and they worked diligently at making the colored paper chains. We draped them over the mantel, and around the living room. We cut out paper Christmas trees, wreaths, stars, and candles. I loved seeing Susan's enthusiasm when I showed her a new decorating idea. Peter and Juliet quickly joined Melissa in the unusual activities, while Nekessa and Otiga delighted in undoing everything. There may not have been any traditional decorations, but by the end of the week our house had been transformed! Transformed into what was probably a real question, but we were all happy.

Two days before Christmas, Otieno eased into the kitchen with "I've got a fantastic idea" expression all over his face. I pretended not to notice. His amazing ideas usually meant that I'd have to learn to adjust to something. He began sharing his great news, "I've been told a large shipment of flour is arriving tomorrow. I ordered a bag of flour from the Duka Moja." A bag of flour was 12 five pound packets! We would have flour for months. Now that I was prepared, Otieno smoothly revealed the plan that he knew would be difficult for me to swallow. "I want to give the two packets of flour we now have to Terri and Caleb, and Judy and Will. We won't need them since we'll be getting more tomorrow. They don't have any flour, and this would really please them."

Was he delirious from a fever? "Give my flour away? Maybe one of the children, but not the flour!" I knew I would be safe with this alternative, because he'd never give the children away. But if Otieno decided to do something, he would do it using such charm and persuasion that it would appear to be the right decision. So I gave the flour away with the confidence that I would have an abundance of flour the following day.

Tomorrow came, but the flour didn't. We were told it definitely would arrive that evening or early the following day. That's the reason I was walking into town on the 24th of December. I was determined to buy flour, so I finished my coffee and returned to my mission.

As I walked along the red dirt road I thought about tomorrow, Christmas day. I had small, used gifts from the Women's League sale for all the children except Melissa. I had nothing for her, and I didn't know what to get. She had experienced the extravagant Christmases we celebrated in America. How would she respond to this Christmas? It would be the first Christmas celebration for Susan, Peter, and Juliet, so anything would be special to them. Otiga and Nekessa were young enough that they would be thrilled with anything to unwrap. I would look in the dukas for a gift for Melissa, but I knew what I would find;

rubber balls and crayons. There wasn't a large toy selection in this small town.

I looked over my shoulder at Kessy, now sleeping peacefully on my back. She loved this trip and the security of being close to me. We had passed the horrible smelling tanning factory, and we were now at the Salvation Army's school for the blind. This was the home for many African albino children who lacked the melanin pigment, which protects the skin, hair, and eyes from the sun's ultraviolet rays. The children's sight is affected and their pale white skin and hair is extremely susceptible to severe damage from the sun. They were outside playing now, in the early morning, before the sun became their enemy.

The trip had gone quickly. I stepped onto the sidewalk that ran directly above the open sewers. Sidewalks meant we were officially in town. While I was here, I would buy the other supplies necessary for our Christmas dinner. Susan, Peter, and Juliet had never eaten fried chicken, mashed potatoes, and gravy. I was sure they would enjoy it. One of Otieno's friends was bringing two prepared chickens (meaning killed and cleaned) into town for us. I was to pick them up at the butcher shop around noon. I didn't mind spending the morning in town. I could cruise the shops for gifts and visit with the storekeepers. I went directly to the Duka Moja where I was to pay for the reserved flour.

"It hasn't arrived yet," the owner told me. "Maybe in the afternoon. Come back then."

The next stop was the butcher shop to buy the chickens, but a stunning light brown Somali woman informed me, "No chickens have been delivered today, and I don't expect any more deliveries."

The tension was beginning to build. I drug my dusty feet to the post office where the only public phone was located. There was always a long line outside the bright red phone booth. When Otieno finally answered, his voice sounded preoccupied. His tone softened as he heard my story, and his response was gentle and caring. "I'll be there as soon as this pineapple crisis is over. Wait for me in town, Carole. I will take care of this."

I continued to check back at the Duka Moja throughout the afternoon, but the flour never arrived. Neither did the chickens. It was 4:00 P.M. when Otieno was dropped off in town. By 5:00 P.M the shops were closed and we both had surrendered to the truth. There were no chickens and no flour. We were sitting at a sidewalk table, looking and feeling very defeated, when a British co-worker of Otieno joined us. He had just sent his wife back to England for the holidays, so he was delighted to spend time sitting and chatting with us. Otieno shared our plight with John.

"Hey, we've a packet or two of flour at our compound. My wife's not going to be using it, since she's in England. Let's have supper, and then I'll run you over to my place to get it."

As we were sitting there listening to one of John's infamous stories, another Del Monte worker and his wife joined our table, and our conversation. "We'll give you a chicken," they immediately offered, when they heard our problem. "We have lots of chickens running around our house."

I couldn't believe what I was hearing! I had spent all day in town looking for Christmas dinner. Otieno had also failed. However, within two hours, dinner had been completely supplied by friends and acquaintances. I knew the source of this blessing, and thanked Him. God was continually showing us His faithfulness. His love and lessons were more personal since I had come to Africa. I was humbled and grateful.

Everyone loaded into John's station wagon and we headed down the dirt road. We slowed down only to carefully pass a barefoot man who was pulling a heavy cart in the road. We stopped at the first house to pick up the promised fowl and to drop off its owners. With a large, live chicken secured between Otieno's arms and legs, we rode on to John's house to get the "golden gift" of flour.

We left the bird in the car and trudged up the grassy hill that was part of the landscape surrounding his rambling old stone house. We entered through an ancient wooden door that led into a spacious country kitchen, smelling of aged wood and a bouquet of savory meals that lingered in the room.

John was busy looking for the flour in his kitchen cupboards when I spotted a mother cat in the corner feeding her kittens. They were tiny, fluffy, tiger kittens with big green eyes. John saw me admiring the babies, and casually offered, "Why don't you take one home to the children. We're overrun with the beasts." My heart leaped with joy! The perfect Christmas present for Melissa! She would love a kitten. While I cuddled the little ball of fur, I couldn't tell who was purring louder, the kitten or me.

As we attempted to get Kessy, the kitten, and ourselves into the car, the chicken escaped! Otieno, realizing tomorrow's dinner was running away, made a heroic dive to recapture the fowl. He missed the bird, and went tumbling over a hedge, and down the hill. After several unsuccessful attempts, he caught the chicken, and returned it to the car. He was out of breath, and quite dirty, but a proud victor.

When we arrived home, I gave the chicken and the kitten to our ayah. I asked her to hide the cat in her room, since it was separated from the rest of the house. This would keep Melissa from seeing or hearing it. She wanted to clean and prepare the bird the next morning because it was the custom to kill the chicken the same day it was to be eaten. Later that evening, after the younger children were in bed, Susan, Melissa, and I began the Christmas baking. There was excitement in the warm air as we introduced Susan to this new experience. I collected all the ingredients, and instructed Susan to get the baking sheet out of the large, lower cupboard. She opened the cupboard door and out walked the chicken. The ayah had stored it there until morning. "What a crazy life," I laughed to myself as I chased the chicken around the kitchen. Once it was secured in the ayah's room, we began making cookies again. We were cutting out the sugar cookie shapes, when I heard a faint drum beat in the distance. It seemed to be growing stronger and closer. Soon there was a small group of African men standing outside our house, singing and beating drums. They were Kenyan Christmas carolers. I didn't recognize the words, or the tune, but their joyful sounds were heavenly. This was the perfect ending to an extraordinary day.

Christmas came early in Kenya, just as it does in America. Our family was unable to sleep past dawn. Everyone was delighted with the presents, especially Melissa. She whispered in my ear that morning, "Mommy, this is the best gift I've ever had." I wondered if the hot African sun had melted her memory of the Christmas presents from the past, but she seemed sincere as she cuddled with her little furry friend.

That afternoon our six children, Otieno, the ayah, and I feasted on one chicken, mashed potatoes, gravy, homemade cinnamon bread in the shape of a wreath, and Christmas cookies for desert. I never understood how one chicken could feed nine people, but it did. Peter and Juliet had "seconds" by chewing on the neck and the feet.

In church that night, as our over-grown family bulged out of both ends of the rustic wooden pew, I realized that some of God's sweetest miracles are in the small and simple things. He provided one small chicken at the last minute, and then multiplied it to feed our masses. He shared Christmas carols sung in Swahili and accompanied by a drum teaching us that love can conquer any language barrier. Through a kitten, I discovered that a child's joy is not determined by the number of presents under the tree. Jesus had met our needs in ways that I would never forget. Christmas took on a richer meaning as we shared this special day with our new children. A spark had been lit within them. Now I understood why the children had come home with us. God had all of us in His hands, and He was blessing us.

# CHAPTER 5: THE PYTHON

## *So Many Tears*

With Christmas over, it was time to get serious about raising our six children. Otieno wanted to register Susan, Peter and Juliet in school when the new term began at the end of January, so it was important for them to learn English quickly. Each morning after we finished the chores, the children and I would settle down on the hill behind our house to "exchange languages." We began with words we could point out to each Other. I'd point to my eye and say, "eye," and then one of them would say "eye" in Abaluhya. It was like a game, and everyone learned rapidly. The bonds of love between us grew as quickly as their mastery of the English language. It was so peaceful during those days. I couldn't believe that caring for six children could be so much fun! We made games out of everything.

We helped Otiga and Juliet conquer their numbers and alphabet by writing them on the cement patio with a soft rock. Peter was exceptionally fast at learning. He was excellent in math, and never wearied of homework. He was devouring the children's pictorial Bible I had purchased for them. Susan had more difficulty with her studies, but she was blossoming in the kitchen. She had become my constant companion and a loving daughter.

On warm afternoons while Susan and I were preparing meals, the little ones would run around the compound. The yard was large and hilly and it was an exceptional playground. The children were creative in their play, inventing new forms of tag, or imaginary battles. They didn't have pre-fab toys, so they made their own. Peter, like many Kenyan boys, shaped coat hangers into the outline of an automobile that he could drive like a toy car. It was an amazing creation. Peter and Juliet's once expressionless faces now beamed. They had come alive, and it was awesome to witness this transformation.

Some afternoons we would walk across the road and through the golf course to the Country Club to swim. Life was such a contradiction for us financially. We couldn't afford to buy "things," or most American foods like tuna, spaghetti, and cereal, but we had an ayah, an askari, a gardener, and we belonged to the Country Club! It was extremely difficult to understand our economic level, so I decided not to worry about this dilemma. I just replaced tuna and cereal with lazy afternoons at the pool.

This peace and serenity were shattered one afternoon when Melissa came running into the house screaming, "Mommy, Mommy, my kitten, my kitten!" I tried calming her so I could discover what was wrong. She was sobbing as she spoke, "A big snake ate my Cinnamon." Nothing could console her. She had just seen a python slither down a tree and swallow the baby kitten she had received for Christmas only weeks before. The eyes of a little girl should never be exposed to this nightmare making image. It hurt her so much, and the other children hurt for her. They were definitely melting into a loving and caring support system for each other.

Soon after this trauma, my world was also ripped apart. We were still living in our house next to the Country Club. I awakened just before dawn. Something was wrong, but I didn't know what it was, or why I felt this way. Otieno wasn't in bed, so I got up to see if he was all right. He was nowhere in the house, and the back door was open. My heart raced because robbers were so common here! I looked outside. The sun had barely stained the sky. Through the haze I saw the ayah's door ajar, so I hurried across the dimly lit patio to her quarters. As I reached her door, I saw Otieno approaching her bed, dressed only in his briefs.

Sabah's eyes were fixed on him, and she smiled a willing smile as he moved closer to her. As his body touched her bed, my eyes met Otieno's eyes in one frozen moment of horror.

Feeling like my kitten had just been eaten by a python, I fled from the door. My heart was broken. He had left our bed to go to hers! Why had he done this? I thought we were happy in all areas of our marriage. We had such a satisfying love life, never routine or stale. I never had headaches or acted uninterested. We had made love that night! "Why?" was all I could think.

She was his relative, and she was only eighteen years old! I couldn't face him, and I couldn't stop crying. I was so ashamed, but why? Why was I ashamed? I had to leave, but I didn't know where to go and I had no way to get there. The children weren't awake yet, so I pulled on my clothes and ran out of the house. My eyes couldn't bear what they had just seen. I needed to close them and make the images go away. I ran until I came to a high grassy area and threw myself on the ground. All I could think was: "Why? Why? Why?"

A black hole of loneliness devoured every part of me, and there was no one I could turn to, so I just stayed there and cried. I don't know how much time had passed when I felt a hand touch my hair, and a deep voice whispered, "I'm sorry."

"Why?" I sobbed, without looking up at him.

"I don't know," he answered, as he sat down in the grass beside me.

"I thought I satisfied you. I thought that I pleased you."

"You do, you always have, and you always will," he said.

"Then, why? I don't understand."

"I don't know, I don't know," faded into the air. "I know that's not a good enough answer, but there is no good answer, is there?" he said, without allowing me to respond. "I'm sorry, and I love you, Carole," he whispered. "I know you don't believe that, but I do."

He was right, I didn't believe him. I wanted to, but I couldn't. We stayed there in the grass all morning and part of the afternoon. I didn't know where else to go.

There would be no answers, only questions beginning with "why"? I didn't leave him that day because I couldn't. I had no place to go. I had to either stay and live with the anger and pain of his betrayal or forgive him and try to mend the huge hole that had been ripped in my heart and in our marriage. I needed to believe him. I let him convince me that he did love me, and that this would never happen again. He sent the ayah away, and found an older, married woman to replace her. It was over. I had to believe this. I had to let go of this unspeakable moment if we were to continue our life together.

The fire God was using to purify and shape my life was growing hotter. He hadn't caused my pain, but He was using it to show me His faithfulness during this time of betrayal.

# CHAPTER 6: JOGO-KAMAKIA

## *So Few Books, So Much Learning*

One afternoon Otieno returned home earlier than usual, looking very upset. The company was not pleased that they were renting an apartment for us and we weren't living in it. It was time for him to swallow his pride and move. Besides, it was a waste of our money. These apartments were located next to the Jogo-Kamakia Hotel.

Jogo-Kamakia was a very successful, older businessman from the Kikuyu tribe. He owned a fleet of buses, a flock of women, an old stone hotel left over from the years of the British influence, and the apartments that we were moving into. He was in the process of building a new modern hotel next to the old one, but it was questionable if it would ever be completed.

His women lived in a collection of little one-room residences, sufficient for their work. When business was slow, they would go over to the hotel to socialize. The hotel had a mammoth party/game room equipped with dartboards, aging wooden tables and chairs, with native music and local beer adding a festive feeling to the drab cement walls and floors. Most of the construction workers who were working on the new hotel lived around the hotel in tin shacks quickly assembled for their temporary shelter. These men were easily drawn to the sweet smelling women, loud music, and strong drink that called to them through the open windows. The compound was always alive with activity. There were goats, chickens, dogs, and cats roaming around the dusty grounds.

The goats and cats were most comfortable sitting on, or walking over, the hoods of the cars. Jogo-Kamakia could often be found sitting on the large wrap-around stone porch that was attached to the decaying building, while his employees catered to his every whim.

I viewed moving to Jogo-Kamakia as an adventure, and that was exactly what it turned out to be. The décor in our new three-bedroom apartment was a vision! All the doors were bright lime green, while the rest of the woodwork was peacock blue. The living room floor was large red and white linoleum squares, creating the feeling of being a part of a huge chess set. The bathroom was equally colorful. It was a long room completely covered with ceramic tile. Unfortunately, the tile was every imaginable color, shape and size, creating a tile showroom effect. The bathroom was bright and colorful, but rather difficult to decorate. The orange tile seemed to be at war with the soft pink, while the small pale yellow squares seemed overpowered next to the large turquoise tile.

There was a small balcony extending off the living room of our second story residence. While Otieno was at work, the children and I would spend many evenings sitting there, just watching our little world. This was an opportune place to learn about the environment. There was an interesting trash disposal system in the neighborhood. An eight-foot cement wall with a tall metal gate stood guard around our complex. This large wall was the Dumpster. The residents merely carried their trash to the wall and tossed it over. The weeds and bushes on the other side swallowed the trash, concealing it from the road.

Instead of an ice cream truck visiting the neighborhood with frozen treats, a small pickup truck came through every few days with glass bottles of milk straight from the cow. We would boil or freeze the milk to pasteurize it so it was safe to drink.

The location of our apartment turned out to be very convenient for us. Susan, Peter, and Juliet were enrolled in the Thika Memorial Church School, which was adjacent to the Jogo-Kamakia complex. The children could easily walk to school each day.

Thika Memorial Church School was one of the better local schools in Thika. Many of the Kenyan businessmen who were unable to pay the large school fees of Imani (the private school operated by Del Monte), sent their children here. Thika Memorial had been the original location of Imani. When Imani moved onto the plantation, the Anglican Church, which was also situated on this compound, took over the school. It was a strategic location, and Thika Memorial prospered. A collection of cement buildings was left over from the original school, and a few small wooden classrooms were added as the school expanded. Across from these buildings was the aging mother church, a lovely miniature of the majestic old stone churches in England. Next to the church was the headmaster's house. The British had built it long ago, when houses were wastefully large and had servant's quarters attached. It was also stone, and appeared to be a relative of the mother church. This house was later to be our home.

Thika Memorial was a good school for our African children. The competition would have been too demanding at Imani. They needed a slower-paced school to begin their education. We had to enroll them below their grade level. Susan went into standard five (fifth grade), Peter into standard two, and Juliet was placed in first grade. Everyone was excited about beginning school. Since I was a teacher, we lived next to Thika Memorial, and three of our children attended the school, it made sense that I should teach there. I applied and was accepted as the Headmistress of the elementary school. I was to be in charge of the primary grades, while the Headmaster, David Kanga, was over the entire school.

Each morning I had a kindergarten class, and in the afternoon, I was to teach a third grade music class and a sixth grade Bible class. In exchange for this, I would receive 1,300 shillings a month (about $130), obviously a meager salary by American standards, but excellent pay in Thika. I could have made much more at Imani, but here I would be near my new children, our home, and the local population.

I began teaching in January, on the first day of the second semester. The students had been on holiday for a month, so they were excited as they entered our little wooden classroom. Since I had never taught kindergarten, and I had thirty children in my class, this should have been a huge challenge. It was however, a heart warming, soul inspiring experience.

As I watched the little ones hop, skip, and stumble into the classroom, one little girl captured my attention. She had a proud walk. This five year old knew who she was, and she was pleased with herself; but she seemed uncertain about me. "I am Muthoni, and I have chocolate and chapati for tea time today." She carefully pronounced each word as she smugly stared into my eyes to catch my reaction. She knew chocolate was a status symbol. I cooed the word "chocolate" to assure her I realized the importance of the statement. She was probably a shopkeeper's daughter. Her English was excellent for a five-year-old. "Are you my teacher?" she asked with concern in her voice. "I've never had a musungu (white or foreign) teacher," she added, without waiting for my answer to her question.

More children cautiously entered the room, and Muthoni began shoving them into the seats around her, making sure to inform each one that she had chocolate. I listened as they greeted each other. Some spoke excellent English, some whispered to each other in Kikuyu, while others said nothing as they timidly melted into their chairs.

Suddenly there was a classroom full of five-year-old children waiting, not so quietly, for me to assume my responsibility as their teacher. As I looked out over the classroom, their small anxious faces caused me to question my ability. Some of the children couldn't even speak English, but I had thirty eager students, and …I searched the small classroom filled only with wooden desks and chairs. We had no books, or any other educational learning equipment. Trying to be positive, I took a quick inventory of what we did have: a box of used pencils and broken crayons, and a small plastic pencil sharpener. The single bare light bulb hanging overhead was much too dim to properly light the classroom.

My eyes dropped from the light bulb and fell upon the children. The light in their eager faces blinded me so that I could no longer see the meager surroundings. I looked into little Muthoni's eyes. They shouted that she was ready to learn to read and write. She didn't understand that we needed better lighting, books, and an alphabet chart across the wall. She had come to school to get an education, and she was waiting for me to begin teaching. That was enough incentive. It was time to begin.

We started class each morning at 8:30. We would form a circle in the school yard and sing songs for about ten minutes. Their favorite was "I'm a soldier in the army of the Lord" because they loved to act out the verses. During the dry season, the red dirt playground was perfect for all of our outdoor activities. We stirred up buckets of red dust that lightly covered everyone like powdered cinnamon over brownies, but no one cared.

However the rainy season created quite a different picture. For weeks our wooden classroom was under attack by the constant deluge of rain and red mud. The children couldn't go out to play, but the mud and rain came inside very easily. Our classroom was situated at the bottom of the hilly school yard, so during the downpours, the mud slid downhill until it landed in the classroom.

The windows had no glass, so the wet rainy days were really wet for us. I was constantly amazed that their little spirits were never damped by the weather or by all of the other difficulties they faced. The children were such a joy to teach, because they were so eager to learn. Discipline was never a problem and nothing seemed to discourage us.

Melissa and Otiga had been at Imani since October, and both were happy and excelling in their work. Melissa was taking horseback riding lessons and was now on the school swim team. She had worked her way up to the third seat in her class. She loved the school, the students, and the lunches. Her favorite was hot, spicy chickpeas. After she had been at Imani for a while, I noticed that her world was expanding, as she interacted with students from Scotland, England, Uganda, and Australia. Otiga was in preschool and he never tired of telling me about his daily adventures and accomplishments.

Susan, Peter, and Juliet were working hard at Thika Memorial. They were also blossoming in their new life. Everyone had chores at home, but there was still a lot of time to play. It was nice having our ayah to help with the household responsibilities. She stayed while I was at school then returned to her family each evening. She would wash the clothes by hand, help keep the house clean, and watch little Kessy.

Everything seemed to be working out very well. All the children had been transplanted successfully, and they were thriving. Otieno's dream had been fulfilled; he was home again. My heart was healing. It is good that God does not allow us to see too far into the future.

# CHAPTER 7: OTIENO

## *So Many Whys*

Each morning as a new day began; my appreciation of the beauty all around me was renewed. Here, I wasn't distracted by the amazing structures of glass and steel that almost touched the clouds, or the miniature towns called malls that had everything I wanted, and thought I needed at 50% off. There were no diversions demanding my attention, so I could enjoy the rooster faithfully announcing the arrival of the sun. There was a coffee plantation near our apartment. Sometimes after dinner, one or two of the children and I would walk there, so they could share school stories without interruptions. Having a coffee plantation near us was nice because there was never a shortage of strong, rich Kenyan coffee. Since our windows were usually open, the alluring aroma of the coffee brewing each morning would float out into the compound, as the sweet scent of the flowering trees drifted in. When we had flour, I'd make stacks of pancakes in the morning and the children would take leftovers to school for teatime. With six children and one bathroom, life was never boring. It was often hectic, but never dull.

Otieno was doing well at Kenya Canners, but now and then he seemed dissatisfied. Occasionally he would share some of his concerns. Coming home was not as he had imagined it would be. We had given up so much to return to his native land, and I believe there were times that he questioned this decision. Otieno missed the luxuries we had left behind in America. He had enjoyed the "things" America had to offer.

Also, in America he was special, but now he was just another African trying to get ahead. This growing unrest in him began to surface regularly.

One afternoon, the children and I were home from school varnishing a kitchen table that Otieno had just built. He was a master at building furniture, which surprised me because he didn't have any experience or training in this craft. When he entered the apartment, he looked troubled about something, so I left the varnishing and joined him in the bedroom.. He was preoccupied and sullen, so I asked, "What's wrong, you look upset."

Instead of answering me with words, his face filled with rage, and he struck me with all the force of his powerful fist. The side of my head was the target of this tidal wave of anger. I vaguely remember awakening for moments throughout the night. It was like coming in and out of a continuing nightmare. One of the children was beside the bed, but I couldn't speak. I tried, but my words were lost somewhere and I couldn't find them. I remember thinking that I needed to get up, but my body wouldn't obey my commands. I didn't realize I was hurt. I just felt as if my mind had left my body, and the two were no longer working together.

Sometime later I heard Otieno's voice fading in and out. As his face and words slowly came into focus, I heard him ask, "Are you OK? Should I call a doctor?" I wondered why he would want to call a doctor, and why I wouldn't be ok. Otieno seemed very worried about my wellbeing. I was unaware that as I passed in and out of reality, nearly eight hours had slipped by. As he continued to quiz me, I remembered. Once more all I could say was, "Why? Why did you hit me?" Otieno had a quick temper, but I had never been afraid of him. It made no sense at all. We hadn't been arguing. He never said why he was angry, he just repeated over and over, "I'm sorry, Carole. I'll never hurt you again. I'm sorry; please know that I am sorry." I was incredibly tired, and I stayed tired for days. Once again, I felt ashamed that this had happened to me. I just wanted to sleep but I had six children who needed me to stay awake.

Otieno was becoming more and more difficult to understand. At times, he was a loving, caring, husband and father. Then, for no reason he would transform into an unpredictable, explosive volcano of anger. The stability of our family's happiness seemed to center on Otieno's moods. If he was content, we had an enjoyable time, but now there was an ever-present fear within me. When would he erupt again?

One afternoon, a few weeks later, Otieno exploded again, but this time Susan felt the force of his unstable temper. She was fourteen, but she had the social maturity of a child. Susan was three years below grade level, and I felt her main job was to go to school and learn all she could. Her classmates were eleven or twelve, but she fit in very well with them. Unfortunately, when Susan would run and play with our children, it would sometimes irritate Otieno.. The peace of this carefree day was shattered when he came home and saw Susan playing tag with her brothers and sisters. A flash flood of insults suddenly poured out of him. Then from nowhere came his powerful hand, smashing into Susan. The verbal abuse was in Abaluhya, but the violence transcended the language differences.

Without thinking, Peter and I rushed to Susan's rescue. I tried to stop him, and Peter went to Susan's side. This was a mistake! After shoving Peter and me away, he lashed out with even more anger at Susan. She didn't cry as she ran away.

I was extremely upset that I had let this happen to Susan! I was her temporary mother, in place of Akinyi. For days I chastised myself for allowing Susan to be hurt.

Then I realized this was wrong. I hadn't let it happen; I just wasn't able to prevent it from happening! Susan belonged to Otieno, just as I did. I had no more say in how he treated Susan than I did in how he treated me. He believed I had no right to interfere in Susan's life, and for me to do so would just make it worse for her. Susan instinctively understood this and she never intervened when Otieno chose me as a target for his wrath, because she knew that would also make it worse for me.

I tried to understand Otieno's behavior. I knew that violence was a part of his upbringing. He had been severely beaten as a child. His mother was almost beaten to death by his father because he blamed her when Otieno became ill. Then a sickening realization interrupted this memory. He was selective with his brutality. He had never spewed out his violence at work or with his friends. It was saved for his family. What if Otieno's anger was like a cancer growing in him? He had recently lashed out in rage at Peter for taking too long to get his newspaper.

Would he choose to hurt Melissa Juliet, Otiga, or Nekessa? All of this was unthinkable; but I must think about it because I couldn't let it happen! However, I knew that I could never stop him from doing anything in his country, where I had no rights and no family to protect and shelter us. An unbearable truth pierced my heart. Otieno should have been our protector and our safe place to go when we were afraid, not the source of our fear.

As the passage of time allowed these nightmares to dim, the pleasant thoughts of my energetic children would flow back into my mind. Play time was very valuable to them and they never squandered it. They knew how to pack in the fun each day. Shoes and electricity were not needed. Cookies and hugs were.

There were also many playful days with Otieno. His fever for life was infectious. Sometimes he would leave work early just to be with me. We would play like children without shyness or reservation, chasing each other through the apartment. Other times we'd just be together, talking and sharing the highlights of our day. One of our favorite activities was dancing. When he and I were dancing, we moved as one body. It took no words to communicate the next step. His body turned, and mine responded instinctively.

This hopeful optimism was my coping mechanism to cloud over the painful reality. I saw no way out of this recurring nightmare, so I had to believe that the good times were a sign that the bad times were over. Allowing the moments of his rage to fade was an imaginary escape from the truth, but it wasn't going to get better, no matter how much I wanted to believe otherwise.

One afternoon Otieno and I were preparing to go to Nairobi for dinner with friends. Both of us were excited about the evening. We had reservations at Carnivore, a popular, upscale restaurant that served many choices of unlimited roasted meat. I was especially excited about getting dressed up and going to Nairobi in a car. I was getting the children settled for the evening, and making sure they had what they needed for the next day, as I said to Otieno, "I just took five shillings from your change box. Melissa needs it for school tomorrow."

This had never been a problem before, but today was different. He turned around, facing me with hatred pouring out of his eyes. "Put the money back," he hissed, as his body coiled and his foot struck me. I was hurt badly, both physically and emotionally. My tailbone was probably broken. After the attack, he was calm again, and very attentive. There was no anger left in him, only remorse. No explanations, only, "I'm sorry, this will never happen again. Please forgive me, I love you." We didn't go out that night.

I had trouble forgetting. The physical pain remained with me, reminding me of the attack. It continued to hurt even more in my heart. Once again, I wanted to believe this would never happen again. I had to believe to be able to go on. I had no place to go, and no one to turn to. I knew I was growing weaker. I prayed daily. I needed help. I needed a friend.

A friend was waiting for me, just beyond the eight-foot fence, and across the road. There was someone who could help me, and I was about to meet this special family. We were attending the beautiful little stone church next to the school. Otieno occasionally joined us, but the children and I attended regularly. There were natives and British attending this Anglican Church, and there was one family from America. We immediately "clicked" when we discovered each other. Their names were Dan and Cathy Schellenberg, and they had four children; Christy, John, Karen, and Sara. Missy already knew their daughter Christy from school. Dan and Cathy were Baptist missionaries from Texas, but both of them had been raised in Kenya by their missionary parents. Finding them was like discovering a cool stream in the midst of a scorching desert. Cathy and I were immediately best friends.

Dan and Cathy had been living in Thika for over a year, and since they each had grown up in Africa, they were at home here. They welcomed their guests with kindness, so that they would also feel at home. Their house enhanced this peaceful ambiance. It was a large open home, not pretentious or elegant, but beautiful in an earthy way.

Dan had made much of their furniture. His simple but sturdy wooden table in the dining room was always a beehive of activity. Dan was a pastor who was able to build, fix, or grow anything.

Cathy was a registered nurse who could paint delicate birds in minute detail or mammoth elephants on a large cloth canvass while we talked and drank tea at their massive table. Dan and Cathy loved. They loved God, and their children, and Africa, and anyone who needed to be loved. They seemed to always have time and space for whomever or whatever God brought into their lives. They had wonderful gatherings on Friday evenings with other families and lots of homemade food, fellowship, and music. They introduced me to an entire network of missionaries from all denominations. God's timing was excellent, because I was about to need a network of prayers.

One afternoon Otieno came home and announced, with much pride that he had a new son, and as soon as the baby was weaned, I would be caring for him. A new son? He told me that Akinyi had just given birth to his baby. He lied to me when he told me she had married another man while Otieno was in America. Lies fell from his mouth like rain from dark storm clouds, and I had been naively dancing and singing in the rain.

The fire within me that once burned for Otieno was being drenched by his lies. Once again, if I could have left, I would have; but I was trapped. I believe Otieno realized this also. I was thousands of miles from home, and I had given up everything to come here. I had to make it! I had children who were depending on me to be there for them.

I believed that Jesus promised not to give us more than we could bear, and I claimed this promise with daily reminders to God that I truly thought I had reached my limit. Otieno never brought the baby to our house, and he never mentioned the baby again. I had no idea what happened, but I knew that I could never question him. I grieved for Akinyi, if she actually was the mother. She had no blame in this. She belonged to Otieno like I did. She had no voice either.

# CHAPTER 8: THE HEADMASTER'S HOUSE

## *So Many Lessons*

One afternoon Otieno broke through the lime green door with the force of a bull, but he wasn't angry. Kenya Canners had agreed to move us out of the apartment and into the headmaster's house, next to the school. David, the Headmaster of the entire school, lived in a house in town, so they rented this majestic stone house for us. They were even sending a team of men to repair and paint the house. Otieno was happier than I'd seen him in a long time. Maybe this move would be a turning point for us! Each day we would walk to the house to survey the progress of the workers. We had applied for a phone, but it would take months to receive one. Another example of "no one ever hurries here."

By this time our furniture had arrived, so we were able to decorate the house very comfortably. At the front there was an enormous stone porch running the width of the house. Leaded glass double doors opened off the porch into a six-foot wide hallway that ran the length of the house. The rooms were spacious, with large windows allowing the beauty of Kenya to pour into each room. There was a stone fireplace in the living room for the cooler July and August nights. White wooden sliding doors opened between the living room and dining room.

There were only three bedrooms, but they were quite large. It was easy to comfortably fit Susan, Melissa, and Juliet into one room, with Peter and Otiga in the other. Otieno built our bed with additional space on one side for Nekessa, so she could sleep nestled next to us, or she could sleep on her trundle bed that fit under the girls' bunk beds. Our bedroom was beautiful. In the center of the largest wall were leaded glass French doors. They were an elegant picture frame for the stone church twenty yards away. I would often stand looking through the leaded glass doors, admiring the splendor of this majestic old building that added charm to the compound. All of the rooms in the house had red cement floors. This was convenient because the floors blended in with the red dirt that was impossible to keep out!

The room we used the most was not even an actual part of the house. Just beyond the dining room was a huge covered screened-in patio. The inside wall of this open area was the house, and the opposite wall consisted of three small rooms, originally built by the British to be used by the ayah. There was a washroom for the laundry, a small kitchen, and the bedroom. All three of these rooms opened onto the screened patio. This multi-purpose room was our favorite place to be. The only piece of furniture was the king-sized table that Otieno built.

Otiga and Nekessa could play while I was cooking or helping the older children with their homework at this table. Since our ayah came to work in the morning, and returned home at night, her bedroom was not being used.

Otieno decided to send for his mother because this would be a comfortable room for her. Having seen her hut, I agreed! Auma's arrival was truly a celebration. Susan, Peter, and Juliet already loved this fragile little woman. Missy, Otiga, and Nekessa were excited about discovering their new grandmother. Her presence was the perfect finishing touch for our new home. She belonged with us, and I hoped she would never leave. Nekessa remained by her side for hours, as though she understood she was Grandma's namesake.

Grandma Auma and I never learned each other's language well enough to carry on a conversation, but Susan, Peter and Juliet would translate for us. In the evenings I would wash Auma's tired, swollen eyes with water, or massage her leather-like back and feet with lotion. She usually sat on a mat on the floor of the screened patio while I was cooking. Once or twice a day she and some of the children would take a walk around the compound. Her favorite activities were to sit outside and watch the children play, and to watch wrestling on television.

TV in Kenya was not like TV in America. There was just one channel, and it operated only a few hours each evening. With permission, the children would pile into our bedroom to watch their favorite programs, usually old American reruns. We continued to invite Auma to join us, but she would always refuse. Her native customs prohibited her from entering her grown son's bedroom, and she was bound by this tradition. The children hated to leave her alone while we were watching TV, so they would run back and forth to her room, sharing the program with her.

Finally, Auma's curiosity was more than she could bear. She entered the forbidden room just to steal a glance at this magic box and she was captured! Her desire to watch wrestling overpowered her fear of breaking this custom. Soon she had moved the rocking chair directly in front of the television so her tired old eyes could catch every move. She still refused to sit on her son's bed, or to be in his room while he was in it. However while he was gone, she spent many hours laughing or shouting at the tiny images on the screen.

Otieno seemed more settled and content after we moved into our house. Once again I eagerly allowed hope to flow back into my heart and I returned to the pleasant task of blending into the community. This was made easier when Judy, also an American wife of a native man from DelMonte, took me under her wing and taught me how to make just about everything that wasn't available or affordable here. With her direction, I mastered crackers, mayonnaise, yogurt, noodles, and brown sugar, just to name a few. She made her own marshmallows, but I never attempted that.

Once or twice a week, Kessy and I would spend an afternoon buying produce at the open market just outside of town. We enjoyed mingling with the women and their little ones as they sat on a mat keeping watch over their fresh vegetables. There were mounds of onions, tomatoes, cabbages, and greens. Baskets of groundnuts (uncooked peanuts), and neat little stacks of dried fish that were next to huge burlap bags of rice, when there wasn't a rice shortage. Bunches of tiny sweet bananas, paw paws, and mangoes were all available for the right price, which could only be determined by bartering.

This slow simple way of life taught me a patience I had never known before. There was no instant anything in Thika. In the beginning, I had difficulty accepting the wasted time spent in waiting for everything, but as my internal clock reset itself to Thika time, I relaxed and accepted the delays of life. Cashing my paycheck was one of my lessons in patience, because this was an afternoon's outing. It would often take hours in the bank to accomplish this chore. I was familiar with banking in America, where people stood politely in line, waiting for their turn. But the rules were different here.

Actually there were no rules. There were no lines. Everyone just came into the bank and pushed and shoved his way to the front. It was complete chaos. I am not a pushy person, so I didn't do well at the bank. In fact I never made it to the front. After much time, I was still standing at the back of this large, packed room. There were no customer service desks to go to for questions. The tellers were at the far end of the lobby behind a wall that had bars all the way to the ceiling. Along the left side of the lobby were also bars that extended from the floor to the ceiling. It looked like a hallway behind bars. As I was looking for a way to move forward, I noticed a teller standing behind the bars at the side of the bank motioning for me to come over. I looked around to make sure he was speaking to me. Going sideways at the back of the bank was much easier than trying to get to the front. I was there in no time. The teller asked me what I needed. I told him I just wanted to cash my check. He smiled a little smile, took my check, and told me to wait here until he returned. Sometime later he returned with my money. He never told me why he did this sweet thing, but from then on, when I needed to cash my check, I just went to the side of the lobby and he eventually came over and helped me.

Almost everything was done slowly in Kenya. Many of the clerks in the stores in Nairobi had never heard the sayings, "Service with a smile," or "The customer is always right." Service just wasn't important. You would get waited on when the clerk was ready, and not before. If she was talking to another clerk, they finished the conversation before waiting on you. It did no good to get annoyed. Service was just like the tempo of the country. No one hurried.

So, I was pleasantly surprised the first time I had to see a doctor. In America it often takes a long time to get an appointment, and once you are there, it is a longer wait. This was not the case in Kenya. One night Nekessa had a very high temperature, and the next morning I decided she needed to be examined. We hadn't been to a doctor yet, so I started searching for one. I was told there weren't many doctors in Thika. There was an aging British man who began "happy hour" much too early in the day, a few Indian doctors, and one African woman. I chose the African woman. It was a good choice. She was an intelligent, informed doctor who took excellent care of Nekessa.

Not only that, but she made house calls. It was so comforting to have the doctor come to your home when one of the children was just too miserable to be moved. Unfortunately, once she got to the house and diagnosed the problem, there weren't many drugs available. She had a sheet with a list of all the drugs. She would go down the list until she found one that was still obtainable and would meet the need. Considering the serious lack of medicine, she was a miracle worker.

One of the reasons the doctor's office was never crowded was that most people went to the hospital when they got sick. I realized this when one of my students told me she had just returned from the hospital. I was terribly concerned until she said she only had malaria and the doctor had given her medicine. "Only had malaria" did not compute with me. I believed it was a dreaded illness because of the death toll from this killer disease. However, "Malaria" was the catch-all phrase for just about every illness to the locals. It was similar to the way we often use the word "flu" in America. If you were sick in Kenya you simply assumed that you had malaria! The hospital was more like a dispensary.

The lines were long, and the wait could be all day, and there wasn't an adequate choice of medicine.

Unfortunately, if someone was really ill and needed extended care, the only place to go, other than Nairobi, was to the hospital in Thika. This was not a pleasant place to stay. It was one big room, with two long rows of beds. Each bed was a metal frame with a thin foam mattress. There were no sheets, pillows, or blankets on the bed. If you wanted them you brought your own, and your family and friends had to bring all your meals to you.

The doctors and nurses had a very difficult job caring for so many people with so little supplies. I'm convinced they were dedicated "angels."

Our family doctor very quickly became a family friend. She had two sons who were five and seven. They were from the Kikuyu tribe, and had lived inland all their lives, so they had never been exposed to the joys of the water. One day I told her that my children and I were off to the Country Club to spend the afternoon swimming. She lit up with an inspired idea. Would I take her sons with me and teach them how to swim? It seemed like a workable plan, until we were all at the pool.

Melissa, Susan, and Peter were good swimmers, but Juliet, Otiga, and Nekessa were still learning. I had trained them never to go into the water unless I was beside them. There was no lifeguard, so everyone was responsible for his own children. This plan had always worked for us, but I wasn't familiar with the doctor's sons. Unfortunately, they had no concept about the dangers of water. I had the five small children sitting on the edge of the shallow end. I would take one at a time into the water for a quick trip across the pool. Each child had been in the water once, and I was starting over, when I noticed the younger boy floating face down. Terror grabbed me and wouldn't let go! I tossed Juliet onto the deck, shouting at her to stay there, as I rushed to the child. He wasn't struggling to stay up. He was just quietly floating face down. I ripped him out of the water, but he didn't respond. I screamed for help, but there was no one near. "Oh, Lord, please help him," I cried, as I laid him down on the warm cement. I had never given mouth-to-mouth resuscitation, but I had taken the course many years before, so I just started doing it. It was as though I was on automatic pilot, because I really didn't stop and think. I just acted. He didn't move for a few moments, and then he suddenly started throwing up water and crying. I had never felt so happy to hear a child cry. I joined him as I held him close to me. "Thank you, thank you, Lord, for saving this little boy." I must have repeated that a hundred times before I calmed down.

We didn't finish the swimming lessons that day, and I never again attempted to teach any children, other than my own, how to swim. The Dr. wasn't nearly as upset as I was, but then she hadn't seen her little boy lying lifeless in the water.

He recovered completely, and I never recovered! I would never forget how God answered my prayer for his young life. The children and I spent many more afternoons at the pool swimming and just enjoying the balmy weather, until the rains began.

This meant it was now time to find an indoor hobby. I had enjoyed baking and decorating cakes in America, so it seemed natural to reclaim this hobby now that I had six children who loved sweets.

I tried to start a birthday party catering service at The Blue Post Inn, but cakes weren't really common, and the people of Thika just weren't ready for this idea yet. Actually, you couldn't buy a cake in the grocery store, and there were no bakeries in Thika. Sweets just weren't as accessible or popular as they were in America, but I was determined to do my part to show these cake deprived people what they were missing!

The catering service bombed, but some time later a storeowner actually asked me to bake and decorate a Cookie Monster cake for him. Maybe if a few people tasted my cakes, they would tell others, and I would be able to create a market in this cake-less society. After all, I knew my African children loved their newly acquired taste for cakes and cookies. So, I delivered the bright blue Cookie Monster to his duka early Saturday morning. The storeowner was busy with customers, but he immediately stopped what he was doing and came over to see what I had brought him. His face broke into a huge smile, and he called his wife out of the back room to see my edible creation.

I waited a few days before I returned to see if his family had enjoyed the birthday cake, and to tempt them with a different flavor for the next one. However, when I arrived at his duka I was stunned to discover they had never eaten a single bite of their cake! Instead, I found it displayed on the ledge over the front window of his shop. Cookie Monster truly looked happy sitting above the window, welcoming everyone into the shop. The owner was quite proud of the new decoration, so I accepted this peculiar use of my cake as a compliment! This idea seemed to catch on much better than the birthday party catering service.

A few months later I had a new cake adventure presented to me by a member of the Women's Club. She had heard from a number of the women that I liked to decorate cakes, and the Club was in need of someone to enter a cake in the National Cake Decorating Contest. Since this was a national competition, women from all over Kenya would be vying for the honor of "Best Decorated Cake."

The only stipulation was that all the materials used must be edible. I was honored that the women chose me to represent them in this contest, but I was surprised that there would even be such a competition. Cakes just weren't a part of this community. Maybe I was judging Kenya by the tastes of Thika? Cakes were probably flowing abundantly in the larger cities, and it would be fun to match my wits against the other cake bakers of Kenya.

I decided I would enter my butterfly cake. I could swirl vibrant colors into the intricate pattern of the butterfly's wings. I followed the symmetrical design of this delicate creature. The wings were an artistic blend of bright blue, lemon yellow, passionate pink, and just a touch of violet. I dyed spaghetti black for the antennae, and rested the lovely butterfly on a bed of grass green coconut.

As with everything in Kenya, it took a long time to hear the results of the contest. One morning, as I was intently teaching the beginning consonant sounds to my 30 five-year-olds, one of the women from the Club walked into my classroom with the long awaited news. I had won Third Place in all of Kenya for my butterfly cake. I was so excited. I couldn't wait to tell Otieno and the children. I imagined how proud they would be of me. Then this sweet deliverer of glad tidings told me the "rest of the story." There had been only two entries in the cake-decorating contest. "Hum... two cakes," I thought to myself. It still hadn't quite sunk in when she explained what that meant. The Other cake had taken first place in the contest, but they felt my cake really wasn't worthy of second place, so they gave my cake third place. It seems the brilliant colors I had used were considered too bright and gaudy.

This vibrantly colored country that proudly displayed peacock blue buildings with flamingo pink trim thought my colors were too bright! We both stood laughing for a long time at the shame of it all. It was good I could laugh at myself, because it took a long time to live down my third place award. I decided it was probably better not to enter any more of my cakes into competition, which was fine with my children. They loved eating them no matter what color they were!

Our lives had been running smoothly since we had moved into the headmaster's house, so when Otieno approached me with a problem one evening, I was totally unprepared. "Carole, I have a kidney infection, and the doctor has given me a prescription for it. He wants you to also take the medicine for a couple of weeks to protect you."

I knew immediately that he didn't have a kidney infection. I looked at him with horror in my eyes, and he knew I understood the truth. The "Headmaster's House" had not been the magic formula for healing the cancer in our relationship. This time Otieno didn't ask for my forgiveness or promise it would never happen again.

The medicine made me ill, and so did the realization that this was never going to end. My skin turned almost gray and I felt drained of life. I just wanted to sleep. Some of these symptoms were due to the shock of the medicine to my body, but my desire to sleep was also due to the pain of his unfaithfulness. Again, I couldn't face this humiliation.

I knew the truth, but I didn't know what to do with it. I began dying inside because it was too painful to live.

After several days of isolation, Cathy came to check on me. I hadn't told the truth about Otieno to anyone. It was time to share this burden before the weight of it buried me. I unloaded my heart and all the grayness that had surfaced to my skin. She listened without judging, and her strength was exactly what I needed. We came up with no answers that morning, but I knew I didn't have to face this fear and humiliation alone anymore. My faith in God had remained strong throughout these traumas, but now God had given me a representative of Himself to help me when I was low on self-esteem and the strength to go on.

Nothing changed much during the next few months. It was a battle to stay above the hurt that was constantly pulling me down. Otieno had not been, was not now, and never would be faithful to me. I needed to face this fact and decide how to deal with it. I couldn't sleep the rest of my life away. Could I fill this emptiness with my children and my students? Once again if I was going to remain in Kenya, I must try.

# CHAPTER 9: JAMES, MELISSA, AND AUMA

## *So Many Challenges, So Much Hope*

JAMES ~

December had appeared on our calendar again, and that meant it was time to celebrate our second Christmas in Kenya. As I sat perched on the stone ledge of our porch and watched the children roll tires down the hill, I took inventory of the extensive plans for this Christmas holiday.

Melissa was leaving at the end of the term to be with her father for a month in America. A gray cloud of concern covered this thought. Missy was only nine years old. Could she fly halfway around the world all-alone? I hated the thought, and for weeks I had tried to justify not allowing her to go. But I had already agreed to this, and she was very excited about seeing her daddy and grandparents. If only I could go with her! But then I'd be leaving the wee ones. She had to go, I had to stay, and I had to accept this or go mad worrying about her.

I left this depressing thought outside to be drowned out by the children's laughter and shouts. It was time to begin getting supper ready. I walked through the house, across the screened porch and into the kitchen. I preferred preparing my own meals. Many of the imported women in Thika left this duty to their ayah, but I truly enjoyed cooking. A larger kitchen would have been nice, or one that was actually part of the main house. I would also have enjoyed hot water in the kitchen; but I had adjusted to these minor inconveniences.

I gathered the vegetables and returned to my favorite room, the large, open screened-in area that connected the house to the servant's area. I enjoyed this no-man's land. Many of our special family times were spent in this simple, breezy area. We were having rice and vegetables tonight. I used to worry when I didn't serve some type of meat, fish, or poultry for our evening meal. In America we would always have some form of meat or chicken each day, but in Africa we rarely had these more than twice a week. I made gravy often, and poured it over bread to go with the vegetables, so the children had the taste of meat and they were able to fill up at each meal.

"Jambo sana, Mama Otiga," flowed through the screen. I smiled at James, our massive askari, and returned the greeting. I wanted to learn Swahili better so I could speak with James as he watched over our family each evening. Since I couldn't talk with him, I put on the stereo. James loved listening to our music. As "Bad, bad, Leroy Brown" cut through the silence, James' entire face smiled as the beat reached him. I sat at the table cutting up tomatoes, onions, and greens, as the younger children danced and sang to the music. Melissa and Susan had gone into town to buy milk and bread. If they could also find molasses and an English chocolate bar, we would cut the chocolate into pieces and make chocolate chip cookies for supper. "Juliet, please go to the kitchen and get the large cooking pot. It's probably sitting on the counter near the stove," I added. Juliet quickly left, and returned even more quickly without the pan. The look in her eyes as she rushed back told me she hadn't returned merely because she couldn't find it.

"Mama, Mama, a big rat is in the pan! Not a mouse, Mama, a Big Rat!" She screamed as she ran. Juliet was not afraid of mice, so I was quite certain she was not exaggerating. Besides, I had seen large rats outside in the open sewers that carried the dirty water out of our house. Seeing a rat outside of the house, and coming upon one, face-to-face in a cooking pot, are two different experiences. As I bravely entered the enemy's camp, I locked eyes with a huge, un-intimidated rat that looked very unhappy with me for disturbing it! I had killed mice before, and even very large spiders, but this was more than I was willing to battle on my own. I cautiously backed out of the kitchen, and gathered the children into a huddle. "Peter, tell James about the rat, and ask him to please come into the house and kill it." Then I gave Juliet her battle command, "Juliet, take Otiga and Kessy into your bedroom, and close the door."

I had done all I could do. It was now time for me to back off and watch. When James understood the problem, a smug grin broke out across his face. Standing proudly, he adjusted his hat and grabbed his club, then smiled one last time as he entered the kitchen, ready for combat. James appeared unnerved; but then so had the rat. Suddenly his Abaluhya words were drowned out by the sounds of crashing pots, and a smashing club.

Before I could find a safe spot to observe this war, the rat and James came bounding from the kitchen in full battle. The rat was well equipped with sharp, ugly teeth, but James seemed to be enjoying the chase. I witnessed one failed attempt at mashing this creature before it disappeared into the hallway.

It was headed for the bedrooms! James apparently needed no further direction, because he was close behind, swinging his club with great gusto. I'm glad I missed the actual battle, because the aftermath was more than enough for me. After many thuds, crashes, and strange sounding words, James exited with his same smug expression, and a broken, bloody rat. He never actually laughed at me, but only because he was a gentleman. He carried the dead enemy proudly, as would a warrior returning from battle. It took James only minutes to be the victor, but it took me hours to clean up the war torn land. There was blood and fur everywhere.

Dinner was a little later than usual that night, but the table talk was full of excitement. Each child told and retold his version of the size of the rat, and the intensity of the battle. James couldn't understand all the words, but he knew he was the hero of the day. He seemed to sit a little taller and prouder as he watched over us that night.

Melissa and Susan had found molasses and a chocolate bar at the duka, so everyone, including James, finished the day with our version of chocolate chip cookies.

## MELISSA ~

Because of the intensity of Christmas preparations, December days are known for melting away much faster than other days. This was happening to our December. It was already time to begin packing for Melissa's trip back to America.

"Mama, I don't have a warm coat. What will I do when I get there?" she asked over and over.

Over and over I answered her, "Anything you don't have, your Daddy will buy for you, dear. He won't let you freeze." She was scheduled to leave Nairobi on Friday evening, have a short layover in West Africa, and then fly directly to New York, where her father was meeting her. It was all so well planned that I should have been calm, but I wasn't.

"Missy, what are you to do when the plane lands in West Africa?" I quizzed her.

Stay on the plane, Mommy," she answered.

"What are you to do when you arrive in New York?" I further questioned.

"The stewardess will take me to Daddy, and I'm not to go to anyone else."

"What if Daddy isn't there?" I continued to drill.

"Stay with the stewardess until he comes or contacts us," she answered routinely, as she looked for pajamas to pack.

I frowned a little less. She seemed ready to go. She had most of the things she needed for the trip, including an elaborate schedule mapping out what she should do at each stop. If all went well, she would arrive in her father's care eighteen hours after she left Nairobi.

Our favorite part of packing was deciding what goodies she should bring back with her. M & M's were the unanimous choice of the children. Susan, Peter, and Juliet didn't even know what they were, but Missy and Otiga had convinced them this was the right choice. We added shampoo, conditioners, lots of Kool-Aid, and some small toys to our important list.

As we remembered things we missed from home, the memories were like old friends we'd left behind: shopping in a mall, watching Saturday morning cartoons, visiting family… It was good that Missy could return home before these memories faded.

"Honey, take lots of pictures, especially of Mom and Dad," I pleaded.

"Mommy, I will, I will. I promise I won't forget to take pictures."

Melissa and I were not in tune for the next few days. I tried to hold back the time, and she tried to wish it away. She won! We were on our way to the Nairobi airport. I reviewed the instructions with her one more time. She sat nervously next to me, trying to hold in her excitement and act very grown-up; so I wouldn't drill her anymore!

"Mommy, who will help you make Christmas cookies?" she asked in a squeaky little voice.

"Susan and Juliet," I answered back. "You can help grandma make cookies this year,"

Small tears formed in the corners of her eyes. "Mommy, I want to go, but I don't want to leave," she blurted out before the tears filled her voice.

I answered silently by nodding my head and reaching for her little hand. She had struggled with the same conflict when we came to Africa and she had to leave her dad.

Otieno took over the conversation. "How about bringing back some Captain Black Gold tobacco for me, and maybe a new pipe?"

As we drove Melissa to the airport in Nairobi, we needed a distraction from our thoughts. God graciously supplied the perfect diversion. There was an extraordinary sunset that evening. The sun was slowly drizzling out of the sky and forming puddles of orange, violet, and cherry along the horizon.

Suddenly, this magnificent picture was filled with large giraffe-shaped splotches. I rubbed my eyes and looked again. Three towering giraffes were actually walking across the road. I couldn't believe it! We had to stop our car to let them pass. To witness such beauty in the wild was a blessing that I would never forget.

We drove into the airport just as the colors faded into the night. So did my heart. The cold imposing terminal loomed in front of us, ready to devour my Melissa.

Otieno took the luggage to be checked in, while I took Missy to the bathroom. As she exited from one of the pay stalls, a friendly bathroom attendant greeted her. There were no paper towels or soap, so this sweet African woman offered Melissa a few sheets of toilet paper as she shook some scouring powder into her hands. It was the perfect way to wash away the loneliness and fear building up within her. Holding in her laughter, she scoured her hands and partially dried them on the toilet paper.

Otieno was nowhere to be found, so I took Melissa to check in. The ticket agent seemed to be a kind and caring man. He looked into our faces and read the worry. As he began processing her ticket he asked, "Would you like to walk your daughter to the plane?

"Oh, yes, may I?" I answered back with relief.

"Actually it would be better if you did," he answered, "because she has a long walk to her plane, and it is quite easy to get confused about which plane to get on. She is really too small to face this alone."

"Thank you, thank you," I whispered to him as I held my little girl close to me. I breathed a sigh of relief as he finished his paperwork, and took us to the Customs Officer.

"This mother will be walking her daughter to the plane," he announced to the official at the gate.

The Customs Officer who had total authority looked at the ticket agent, then looked at us. "No she is not!" he answered, not only in words but with his entire body. "The child will go alone. No one is allowed beyond this point without a ticket."

The ticket agent stiffened as he answered back," I have the right to give her permission to accompany her daughter because she is only a child!" As his volume increased, he pushed Missy and me closer to the gate.

The Customs Officer stood, confronting our red-faced ticket agent, and shouted, "She will go alone, and I will see to it that you lose your job!" As he shot out these words, he angrily pushed Missy through the opening with one hand, and slammed me against the back wall.

Missy was shaking and sobbing on one side of this man, and I was feeling the same way on the Other side. "Mommy, Mommy, are you OK?"

"Don't go near her!" the man's eyes were shouting, as his mouth repeated the message.

I was helpless, and so was she. Our ticket agent pushed past the Customs Officer and held Missy. "I'll take her to the plane," he shouted back to me as he scurried my little girl away. Otieno arrived on the scene just in time to see Missy vanish down the long hallway.

"If I'd been with you, none of this would have happened," he kept repeating all the way home. "I could have walked her to the plane without any problems."

My heart had been smashed when this horrid man shoved Missy through the gate. How could I send my little girl away like this? She would have eighteen hours to be tormented by this trauma. I hated myself for allowing her to fly alone! I hated this insensitive man for creating such an agonizing departure! I hated the thought of her being away for a month, and I wouldn't be able to comfort her. I cried all the way home. Why had I let her go? Sometime during the long dark night a seed of hope began to sprout. I couldn't be with her, but she wasn't alone. I had to believe what I had taught Missy to believe. God is always with you. I had to trust that Melissa was safe in His care!

I also had to trust that Otieno would be safe because he had decided to go to Sigulu Island to plant 300 small trees. This had been a dream of his since we had arrived, and now it was finally coming true. He needed help on the long trip, so Peter and Juliet were accompanying him, while Susan remained with me. We spent hours packing and re-packing the trees and the luggage they needed for a two-week stay on the island. If we hadn't just purchased a station wagon, the project would not have been possible.

It was difficult being away from my family, my country, and now my husband and half of my children. I reminded myself that "difficult" was not a synonym for "impossible." I was learning to turn to God for peace in the storm. I decided this was only a small storm. As I walked back into the house, "Tis the Season to be jolly" was playing on our stereo. I picked up the needle to find a different song, because this season I didn't feel jolly! When the music started again "I'll be home for Christmas" flowed through the air. I took the record off and checked the next title. "I'm dreaming of a white Christmas" brought no comfort. "Not this year," I thought.

## AUMA ~

I sat down on the living room floor. Nothing was the way it should be this Christmas. How could I possibly get into the Christmas spirit? Then little Kessy crept up behind me and pounced on my back. I rolled over and held her close to me. She could always make me smile. Christmas personified was hugging me. This little bundle of love was ready to play. She was happy we were sitting on the floor because that meant fun was on the way. Add Otiga to the picture and we had a party.

Children are such clear thinkers, probably because their minds come pre-programmed with thoughts of playing, laughing, and hugging. They are small compasses for adults, pointing out the direction we should be heading.

If we can't celebrate Christmas with all our family, then we can celebrate with the ones who are here. It was a magnificent plan and little Kessy said it all with just her smile.

As our Christmas plans began to unfold, a star for the top of our invisible tree appeared. It was Grandma Auma. She had existed her entire life with no one ever pampering her. She had lived a colorless life on the island in her small mud hut. She was now old, crippled, and almost blind, but she never complained. It was time someone spoiled her. We had begun this process a few months earlier when we brought Grandma home to live with us. She now had her own room, a real bed with sheets and blankets, enough to eat, grandchildren to love her, and occasionally wrestling on TV.

This would be Auma's first Christmas ever. I had no time left to think about missing anyone as we prepared to make Grandma Auma feel like a queen. I shared my idea with the children, and they loved it. Susan, Kessy, and Otiga began making pictures to hang in her room.

I didn't have much money to spend on a gift, so I had to be creative. A new dress! The few dresses she had were faded and worn. I searched through my wardrobe. It had to be special. My "ceremonial gown" from Kuwait popped out at me. I had received it from a foreign exchange student some years ago. It was a regal, long, tapestry robe, with golden thread woven through it. The bright red, gold, and orange threads were blended together in a pattern truly fit for a queen. Susan found a scarf at one of the dukas with the same colors in it, and I discovered a pair of ear rings in my jewelry box that accented the dress perfectly. The final touch was an almost new purse from my closet. Now none of us could wait until Christmas! We spent the remaining few days hanging homemade decorations, baking Christmas cookies, and pampering Grandma with back rubs.

On Christmas Eve we all went to the service at the little stone Church next to our house. As we sang songs praising our Lord and celebrating His birth, my heart overflowed with the Christmas spirit. Grandma Auma couldn't sing the words, but her face was as bright as the candle she held in her tired hands. After the church service, the Schellenbergs invited us to share in Dan's birthday party. We ate homemade birthday cake, laughed, and talked of Christmases past. Cathy and Dan knew of our plan, so Cathy had painted a small picture of two African birds for Grandma. Love was shared that night. There were no expensive gift exchanges or lavish food, just the joy of being together with friends who shared a love of Jesus and a love for each other.

Christmas morning was even more fun than I had anticipated. The children were all thrilled with their small gifts, but everyone seemed most excited about Grandma Auma opening her presents. The first package she unwrapped was the dress. Her almost dead eyes came to life as they gazed on the beauty of this "royal creation." She immediately put it on, right over her old worn dress. A smile spread across her face like that of a little schoolgirl trying on her first-day-of-school dress. The age lines seemed a little less prominent as she stood there, allowing each of us to admire her beauty. Next, she opened the scarf and earrings. They also went on immediately.

As she opened her last gift, the purse, she began speaking to Susan in their native language. I could tell by her face that this was a very emotional moment for her. After Grandma finished talking, Susan passed her words on to us: "I want to return to my village today so everyone can see me. I would feel so proud. I am ready to die now because I have something beautiful to be buried in." Now she could die without worrying about her clothes. We couldn't have given her a more important gift, other than the peace of knowing that she would go to Heaven and be with Jesus when she died.

With Susan's help translating, we had often talked with her about Jesus. I smiled as I thought about Grandma walking around Heaven with healthy feet and eyes as she gazed with joy at her loving Father who welcomed her home.

That afternoon we ate fried chicken just as we had last Christmas. Grandma had never eaten chicken before. She told Susan she felt guilty because on Sigulu Island women weren't allowed to eat chicken. Only after we promised never to tell the other women in her family, would she try it. She ate two pieces that day, so she must have enjoyed it.

I received my Christmas present much later that night when I finally reached Melissa in America. I had been trying for hours, and I was just about to give up and go to bed. Suddenly the ringing of our recently installed phone broke the silence of this Christmas night. It was the operator saying, "I've finally reached your party, one moment please."

On the Other end was my little girl calling out, "Mommy, is that you?"

"Merry Christmas, dear," I shouted into the static. "I love you and I miss you so much," I added with a shaky voice.

"Oh, Mommy, I'm so glad you called," she repeated over and over. I asked her about Christmas, and what presents she had received. She answered me, and then added with tears in her words, "Mommy, my very best present was your call. That's what I wanted most."

We chatted a little longer, and then we hung up with an "I love you" coming from both of us. I fell asleep on the couch listening to one of our Christmas albums. The last song I remember as I drifted off was, "I wish you a Merry Christmas, and a Happy New Year."

# CHAPTER 10: THE BEGINNING OF THE END

## *So Much Love, No More Hope*

I had been praying for some time that the Lord would show me, without a doubt, what I should do concerning my marriage. I had promised "until death," and I wanted with all my heart to honor this vow. However, there was an internal alarm that kept warning me that I was in serious trouble.

On Saturday night, March 6, 1982, I received clear directions. This particular evening Otieno and I were to attend a dance at the Country Club. There was a production problem at the pineapple plant, so Otieno told me to go on to the Club, and he would meet me there. As he walked into the Club later that evening, I could see he was angry. This was so often the case lately that I had learned not to question him because it just infuriated him further.

I felt my body begin to tense. "Please don't be mad tonight," I thought to myself. This was our evening out together. I tried to appear oblivious to his disposition by smiling as I walked over to him. This was not the acceptable response tonight. My smile just added fuel to the fire that was already raging within him. I sat quietly waiting for a clue that might help me know what I should or shouldn't say. I felt such confusion and helplessness at these times.

Otieno took my hand and led me to the dance floor as a new song began playing. Maybe the music would help release some of the tension that was captured in his body and was seething out of his face.

Before I realized what was happening, Otieno had danced me from the Clubhouse and onto the deck of the pool. Then he stopped dancing and held me at arm's length. I looked at him, trying to understand what was happening. "You're going to leave me, aren't you?" flamed from his mouth. "You're planning to go back to America, I know you are!"

I started to speak, but his eyes filled with fire from the words he spoke, and then his fist became ignited, and he smashed it into the side of my head.

"No, not again! This can't be happening again," was all I could think; as I fell to the ground and covered my face. This was like throwing gasoline on his raging fury. He grabbed my head with his hands, forcing me to look up at him. His smile was evil and sadistic. He was enjoying this moment! He spoke slowly, savoring every word he spewed out at me. "It is my right as your husband to beat you any time I want, and this will happen again!" He laughed. "And if you continue to cry, causing a scene, I will create an even greater scene by drowning you in the pool." I knew he was serious, and he possibly was hoping for the opportunity to fulfill this threat.

At this precise moment everything became completely clear, as though the darkness and confusion were suddenly overcome by the light of this truth: Otieno was not going to stop hurting me. If I stayed with him, I would be choosing a life of physical and emotional abuse. It was not going to get better; it was only going to get worse.

Otieno knew what he was doing. I lay on the ground as quietly as I could. If I lived through this night, I knew what I must do. It was as if God was saying to me, "Do you have any doubts about your choices?"

Otieno turned and walked away from me without saying anything else. No one came outside that evening, and no one else was aware of the explosion that went off inside my head. He returned a moment later with my purse. He was now very calm and relaxed as he drove us home. He then fell into a deep sleep.

I awoke the following morning with fragments of a nightmare floating in and out of my mind. As I attempted to focus on this bizarre dream, I realized the pain and fear were not part of any dream, they were real! It was Sunday morning and Otieno was gone, but the image of his face at the pool remained much too vivid. I thought about church, but I was afraid to meet anyone. I was ashamed, and I felt worthless and alone. It would be less painful if I just went back to sleep. It was easier to stay asleep than to face reality, but... once again, life had to go on with me awake.

I helped the children prepare for church. They were unaware of last night's activities, and they were all excited because Melissa was ten years old today, and that meant a birthday cake and a family party. Susan, Peter, and Juliet had learned quickly about the joys of a birthday. They had never experienced birthday cake or birthday parties before they came to live with us. Since none of them knew the actual date of their birth, we chose a day of celebration for each one. I would hide twenty or thirty shillings inside the cake for the birthday child. That would keep them in Coke and chips for a long time. Their favorite game was finding the hard candies I had hidden around the house. Susan would carefully direct little Kessy to her share of the candy because she was too small to find them herself. There wasn't money enough to buy presents, but that didn't matter.

I knew I couldn't allow the violence from last night to show on my face. It would dampen this very special day for Melissa. I also knew the importance of not letting the memory of last night fade with the passing days. I must not forget the look in Otieno's eyes and the promise, "This will happen again!" We must leave; but the planning that it would take to leave Kenya seemed to be an impossible task! With the heaviness of these thoughts on my mind, I began gathering the ingredients for the birthday cake. As I worked I prayed and prayed, "Please, God, help me! I know we are to leave, but I don't know how."

Otieno had taken Otiga's and Nekessa's passports. I remembered how long it had taken to get the passports in America. Everything took longer in Africa, and I wasn't even sure that I would be able to get new ones, especially without Otieno's consent. To withdraw the amount of money needed to purchase four tickets to America would require my husband's signature.

There were different rules here. He was the Kenyan and I was the foreigner. He was the man; I was only his wife. I had no rights and no authority. He had made the children Kenyan citizens, so they had dual citizenship. He had begun locking us in the house at night while he was at work. He said it was for our safety. We both knew the truth. The situation seemed impossible. How could I ever get past all of these obstacles without Otieno knowing? It would take a miracle for us to get out of this nightmare, but… do miracles happen anymore?

My thoughts were interrupted by a voice calling my name. It was Dan Schellenberg. "Hi, Carole. We didn't see you at church, so I decided to stop by and check on you. Is everything all right?"

Dan had never just "stopped by" before. When I tried to speak to him, all I could say between my sobs was, "We must go home, we must go home." His gentle reply was even more puzzling than his unusual appearance at our house. "We've known for a long time that you must leave. We've just been waiting for you to realize it. We'll have you out of here by Monday night. There's no time to spare!"

I had not yet shared why I was so frightened, nor any of the events of last night. How could Dan know I must leave quickly? Who was the "we" he was referring to when he said, "We have known for a long time you must leave." My already overloaded mind broke, and I spilled out all the fears I'd been holding inside. I was emotionally drained when I finished telling him the secrets I had been afraid to share.

Dan looked at me with compassion, but he spoke to me with determination, "I know you realize it's not going to be easy to do this without Otieno finding out, but you must leave, and you must do it immediately!" He seemed to understand the importance of our leaving quickly even better than I did. "You are not to worry about anything," he instructed me. "We'll work out all the details and you're to go on as if nothing is wrong. If Otieno suspects anything, he'll do all he can to stop you. You know that, don't you? Don't tell anyone what you are doing; you can't take any chances."

He walked to the door as he spoke, "I won't be back, but Cathy will keep you informed."

Dan left, and I was in shock. My prayers had been answered! I felt a calm deep within me. I knew I must remain this way for our escape to take place. "Escape!" I had not actually thought of our leaving as an escape, but it was. The only way out of Africa was to escape. The words sounded like a movie plot, but I had no doubt about this being real.

Melissa's birthday was not spent with a birthday cake and a family party as I had planned. Otieno returned home and announced, "I'm taking you and Melissa to the horse races in Nairobi for her birthday. We'll have dinner there, and then visit Ben on the way home. Get ready quickly." I knew the other children would be very disappointed, but I didn't argue.

The afternoon was like a pleasant dream. Had we stepped out of my nightmare and into the world of make-believe? The weather was warm, with a gentle breeze that took the heat from the sun and cooled it to the perfect temperature. We had dinner on the outside terrace, which was artistically framed by flowers of every color, blending softly into one another. No one spoke of last night. It was as though it had never happened.

When he hurt me before, he had been very apologetic afterwards. Today there were no apologies, no anger and no reference to any problems between us. He was kind, thoughtful, and totally pleasant. Was he a Dr. Jekyll and Mr. Hyde, or was I losing touch with reality? I closed my eyes and the dark, ugly images of last night returned. No, I was sane... but was he? How could he be two completely different men within twenty-four hours? We returned home late that afternoon, and Otieno left the house immediately.

I called the Schellenbergs as soon as he was gone. They had gathered many of the missionaries in the Thika area together at their home to organize the details of our escape plan. The missionaries were the "we" Dan had kept referring to that morning. Dan spoke intently to me: "Carole, you are to stay home from school tomorrow. Say you're ill or something. As soon as Otieno leaves the house, call Cathy so she can inform you of our plans. We're trying to get you out tomorrow night."

Monday had to begin as usual, and everything had to remain normal. I pretended to be sick, and sent a message to school saying I would not be there today. I loved teaching here. I didn't want to leave the children. If only I could explain why we must leave. But I couldn't tell anyone.

Cathy called while Otieno was still at home. I told her I was not at school today because I was ill. She offered to take Otiga and Nekessa in the afternoon, so I could rest. I didn't know why she was doing this, but I knew she had a reason, so I accepted her offer. She reminded me to call her later and then she hung up. It was not difficult pretending I was ill. It was, however, difficult to act calm. The day seemed to crawl.

Late that afternoon the car from Kenya Canners came for Otieno. Had I actually concealed my thoughts? I told him Cathy would be bringing the children back home before bedtime. He seemed at ease as he left. I called the Schellenbergs as soon as he drove off the compound. Dan answered, "Carole, I'm coming to get you. Tell the children you're going to Nairobi for medicine, and since Otiga and Nekessa are at our house now, you're taking them, also." I didn't know why I was going to Nairobi, but I followed the instructions.

When Dan arrived, he appeared very concerned. I had never seen him look this way. As he drove well above the speed limit, he told me of the day's activities. "A photographer in Nairobi is holding his studio open until we arrive. He'll make new passport pictures of Otiga and Nekessa. Carole, you won't believe what has happened today." The story he shared explained the anxiety on his face. "Because you are the wife of a Kenyan man you must have his permission to leave the country. You must also purchase a round trip ticket to insure your financial ability to return."

"I can't even leave here without Otieno's approval?" I was beginning to panic. I had to leave!

Dan interrupted me. "I went to one of the government offices to speak to someone about getting the necessary papers to by-pass this requirement. I was waiting in one of the lines for a long time, of course. The line I happened into was manned by a fellow tribesman, so I was able to talk to him in his native language." Dan had been raised in Kenya among the Akamba tribe, and he spoke Kikamba as well as he spoke English. "In researching Otieno's file, he found a number of questionable discrepancies, so he granted the papers for your departure. Carole, he couldn't share the facts with me, but he stressed that you should leave as soon as possible." I listened intently as he continued, "After that, I went to the American Embassy and told them the problem concerning the children's passports. The woman agreed to talk to us after the embassy closes tonight."

We arrived at the photographer's studio, quickly had the children's passport pictures taken, and then headed to the American Embassy. We were to go to a side entrance, not the official front door. An armed guard stood outside this entrance. No words were spoken as he led us up a flight of stairs to a closed door. When he knocked, a woman answered and invited us in. Dan introduced us, and she immediately began asking me questions, "Carole, do you want to return to America?"

"Yes, we can't stay here any longer."

"Do you think your husband might try to follow you?"

"I don't know. It's possible, but I don't know. I know he would try to stop us if he knew we were planning to leave. If he were angry enough, he might try to follow."

She then painted a very explicit picture for me. "You realize it is not customary to issue new passports when the existing ones have not been lost or destroyed. Just because Otiga's and Nekessa's passports are not available to you is not reason enough to issue new ones. However, I have seriously considered the information Mr. Schellenberg presented to me earlier today, and based upon the urgency of this situation I feel I have just cause to re-issue the passports." She smiled faintly as she added, "If you had not registered your passports with the American Embassy when you arrived, this would not have been possible."

My thoughts were jerked back to the last words my father had spoken to me just before we left for Africa, "Carole, the first thing you must do when you arrive in Kenya is register with the American Embassy. Promise me you'll do that." How could he have known the importance of this request?

The woman now spoke to Dan and me. "You both must be aware of the dangers involved in this attempt to leave Kenya. Because your husband has officially made the children Kenyan citizens he could have you arrested for kidnapping if he discovers what you are doing. Dan, you and your wife could also be arrested for assisting Carole. Have you and Cathy considered the consequences of helping Carole and her children?"

Dan spoke without hesitation, "We're both aware of the risk, and we're both willing to take it."

My eyes filled with tears. These people were not blood relatives. We weren't even life-long friends. I had just met them in Kenya, and yet they were willing to put their lives on the line for us. Also, this woman from the embassy had just told me she could lose her job for the decision she had made concerning the passports, but she knew it was the right decision. How could this be? My heart was breaking with the love I felt from them and for them. I didn't deserve all of this love. I could never repay these people for all they were willing to sacrifice. I knew deep within me that this was not an "everyday love."

This was the love Jesus spoke of when He said, "*Greater love hath no man than this; that he lay down his life for his friends.*" (John 15:13) They were living what they believed.

I thought about The Greatest Friend, Jesus; and how He gave His life for me, and I didn't deserve this, nor could I ever repay Him.

The woman from the embassy brought me back into the moment with one final warning, "You will not be safe until the plane is actually in the air. If your husband discovers your plans and alerts the authorities, they can remove you and the children from the plane if it's still on the ground."

We couldn't delay at the embassy any longer than necessary. It would be safer if we arrived home before Otieno came back for supper. As we sped towards Thika, Dan carefully explained the escape plan. We were to fly out of Nairobi at midnight the next day, Tuesday, March 9th. I could scarcely believe this was happening. I thought back over the hurdles we had to overcome in order to leave. The passports were being made and Dan was picking them up tomorrow afternoon. The embassy would attempt to prohibit Otieno from leaving Kenya to go to America, but they could do nothing if he tried to leave from Uganda.

The second problem was financing the trip. Since I was required to purchase return trip tickets, this amount was enormous, and I had no access to any money without Otieno's consent. Dan and Cathy once again gave completely and unselfishly of themselves. They had received money as Christmas gifts from family and friends, and they were using this money to buy our tickets. Three months earlier they would not have had these resources.

The locked doors at night, and James, our askari, were still major concerns. Since Otieno was working nights this week, he should be gone, but he often returned home for supper about the time we would need to leave for the airport.

There were still too many "ifs" to feel confident about the success of our escape. My mind was in a semi-alert state, so I was less aware of the odds. I merely sat in the front seat of Dan's car and inhaled his thoughts and plans. He kept emphasizing the importance of procedures I must not forget. At this moment, I could barely remember what day it was. Now I must be alert and organized or this plan could self-destruct, taking the Schellenbergs, my children and me with it.

I focused on every word he spoke. "Since Otieno knows our car, it will be too dangerous for me to pick you up tomorrow night, so Bill (one of the missionaries) will drive to your house. He'll then drive you and the kids to the Salvation Army Blind School where I'll be waiting. Bill and I will drive you to Nairobi in my car, in case the askari notices Bill's car and reports it. Carole, you are to call our house as soon as Otieno leaves for work tomorrow afternoon. That will start the plan in motion. Don't awaken the children until you call me. You will have one-half hour from that time to get ready to leave." We were almost to Thika when Dan asked me, "Do you have any questions?"

"Yes, can I call my parents and tell them we are coming home?" He hesitated, and then answered, "No, I will call them after the plane takes off. It will be safer, and…" he hesitated again…"if you don't make it out, it would be too difficult for them."

# CHAPTER 11: OUR ESCAPE

## *So Little Time*

Tuesday morning, March 9, 1982. It was almost time. The adrenaline in my body was flowing at peak speed. I felt as though I should be scurrying around, preparing for such a major trip. But I knew I must remain in bed, pretending I was ill. This was to justify the story that I had to go to Nairobi the previous afternoon to get medicine.

Just as a dying man's life passes before him, my life in Thika Kenya was flooding my thoughts. I loved Kenya! Otieno's home and family had become my home and family. I'd never felt more in tune with a culture than I had here. My soul belonged here! I loved the gentle spirit of the children in my classes who always saw the world through hope stained eyes. My days were blessed by the loving and caring women who would see me walking from town and would come just to walk with me or would offer to carry a bag. I would miss the neighbors who would drop by the house with a pot of cooked beans and corn and we'd have tea together as we talked. I was leaving the outdoor market where we would play the game of bartering and each of us laughed as we made the deal that we had agreed upon. I loved the people, our home, the music, the weather, and the slow peaceful tempo of life.

More than anything else, I grieved that I would never again be with my children that I had to leave behind. I belonged with Susan, Peter, and Juliet, and they belonged with me, but there was no way to take them. . Our hearts were going to be permanently scarred. I would never stop loving Otieno's mother. Everything in me grieved because I would no longer be able to pamper her. She was cherished for the first time in her life, and now all of this was being taken away from her.

I knew as I prepared in my mind to leave that much of my heart would never make the trip, but my body had to go. So at midnight tonight, if everything went well, we would be gone. All day I had to hold back the tears that kept trying to give away my secret. It was such a lonely time. It hurt to know I'd never again see the people I'd grown to love so dearly, and that I was not able to tell them "good-bye," or "I love you." It would have been easy to convince myself that I could stay, because surely he would never hurt me again. That's what I wanted to believe. That's what I wanted to do; stay and never be hurt again. But I knew the truth.

I tried to understand what had gone wrong. None of this made any sense. It was Otieno who was unhappy. He hadn't adjusted to the shock of returning home to Africa. He would hint at how much he

missed America, football, our home in Indiana, or Captain Black Gold tobacco.

He seemed to grow angrier each day at his decision to return to Kenya, and I was a living reminder of the life he had left behind. No, that was just an excuse I was making for him! This was his choice and he had made that clear!

Today he was to go to work at 4:00 P.M, as he had done the day before. This meant he would return home for supper at 9:00 P.M., presenting a very real threat to our departure. When he returned home, he would have ample time to begin looking for us. If we chanced waiting until he left again, around 10:30 P.M., we would probably miss the flight. I knew Dan had planned everything he could control, but he could do nothing about the time Otieno came home for dinner. "This," Dan said, "We must leave in the hands of God.

Sometime in the afternoon, Otieno received a phone call from his work. His driver would not be able to pick him up until 6:00 P.M. this evening. I wasn't sure how this would affect our plan, but I couldn't warn Dan of the time change.

As I waited for the afternoon to pass, I tried to soak in some final memories of each child. I called Peter and Juliet to the bedroom to chat. They had grown so much, both socially and intellectually. Peter was such a gentle boy. I knew he loved being with us in Thika. He smiled and laughed often now, and loved to be hugged. He was constantly reading his Children's Bible, and was well established in school. Juliet was still quiet, but she had learned to laugh and play with the other children, and she loved school. She needed more time to develop confidence in herself and to trust others. It hurt too much to realize that our leaving was going to devastate all of them, and I could do nothing to prevent it.

Susan crossed my mind, and panic gripped my heart! She could not be left behind! Otieno would take out all of his anger on Susan. I couldn't take her with me; I had no right to do so, nor was it possible. There had to be someplace she could stay until the storm of his anger blew over. I couldn't risk asking her now. I'd wait until we were leaving, and just take her with us. Surely one of the missionaries would give her shelter for as long as it was necessary.

It was five o'clock, and James, our askari, had just come on duty. He and Otieno chatted in Abaluhya for a few moments, as they often did. It reminded me of the problem that I had not yet solved concerning the locked doors. Soon Otieno would be leaving for work and he would lock us in for the night.

I remembered where I might find a key to the double doors that led from our bedroom directly outside. When the workmen were painting our bedroom they had opened those doors. After they finished the house they left a tin can of keys. We had never used these doors, but maybe the key was in that can. It was a different shaped lock, so it should be easy to find the matching key. While Otieno was outside, I quickly searched through the spare keys in the can. I found one that looked right, but I didn't want to chance trying it in the lock while he could walk in and see what I was doing. I would wait for a safer opportunity.

As the time approached for Otieno to go to work, the tears I had been fighting back broke through. I didn't understand these feelings. I wasn't leaving because I had stopped loving Otieno. I was leaving because I must for my children and me to survive. I wanted to tell him that I had no choice. I wanted to stay here forever, but he had made that impossible.

When he walked back into our room that afternoon, it was as though he read my mind. He closed the door and locked it. I wasn't afraid. I knew what he was doing. It was the perfect way of saying good-bye.

We were awakened by a knock on the door, and Melissa calling, "Mom, Cathy Schellenberg is on the phone." I was confused! Why was it so dark? I looked at the clock. It was a little after eight P.M. What had happened? Why hadn't the driver come? What if he didn't go to work tonight? My thoughts were wild now! I got up and rushed around putting the children to bed. If we were able to leave tonight it would be easier if everyone was asleep. Peter and Otiga were now in their room. Susan, Juliet, Melissa, and Kessy were always more difficult, so I had to be extra firm with them.

Otieno returned from the phone very upset. There had been some mix-up in transportation. They were sending someone immediately. "I'll just grab something to eat now before I leave, because I probably won't be able to get home tonight. They've been waiting for me for two hours, so we'll be behind the entire shift. That stupid transportation department has messed up the entire night!"

As he hurried back to the bedroom to get dressed for work, he shouted back to me, "Oh, Cathy called to see how you were feeling."

The driver arrived even sooner than he had expected. He rushed out, leaving his dinner unfinished. Otieno was in such a hurry that he forgot to lock the door. He didn't even close the door as he hurried out past the askari! One of my major concerns had just been dissolved. Dan hadn't done this. It was as though God was giving us a green light to leave.

My heart was beating so loudly now that I was sure Otieno could hear it. He hadn't locked the door! I called to him as he ran to the car, "Good-bye, I love you." I'm sure he thought I was saying good-bye for the evening, but I knew I was saying good-bye forever.

I took a few moments to organize my thoughts. I walked into Grandma Auma's room to check on her. She was asleep as I whispered, "I wish I could explain, but somehow I know you understand. I'll miss you and I will always love you."

I went into the dining room and called Dan. He was frantic! It was a few minutes before nine o'clock. I quickly told him about the transportation mix-up, and because of this, Otieno would probably not be returning home before our plane took off.

Dan's voice was clear and concise as he gave me the final instructions. "Bill will be at your house at 9:30. You and the children must be ready to walk out as soon as you see his lights approaching. That will give the askari less time to think about what is happening."

I interrupted him with an important question: "May I bring Susan with me? If we leave her, she may get hurt. Maybe one of the missionaries could keep her until Otieno calms down?"

"Of course," he answered. "We'll leave her at the Blind School with the Morrisons." As I was about to hang up, he gave me one last direction, "Carole, you must rip off the phone cord as soon as you hang up. Then if he should return, it will be harder for him to contact the authorities."

It was time for action and I must do my part without hesitation. I hated to destroy the phone; it had taken us months to get it installed. But I knew I couldn't get sentimental now or all could be lost, so I ripped it off.

I awakened Susan first and told her what we were doing. I didn't have time to explain why, but she understood. "Susan," I said quietly, "I want you to leave with us, and stay with some friends until you feel it is safe to return. You may stay with this family as long as you want. You must be strong and help Peter and Juliet be strong. I love you all and, I'm so sorry that we must leave." She nodded her head in agreement, and began helping me. I knew her world was being ripped apart, and I wanted to talk with her about it, but there wasn't time.

Twenty-five minutes isn't much time to awaken and pack three children for an overseas trip. Melissa, who was usually the most stable child, began crying because she was afraid. "Mommy, what if Otieno finds us? He'll be mad. Please, let's wait until it's safer to go. I'm so scared when he is mad at you."

"Melissa, we must leave tonight. You are to hurry and pack the things that are most important to you, and pack your best clothes." She started to argue with me, but I interrupted her. "There is no time to discuss this, Missy. You must do as I say, now!"

We were not ready when the car lights appeared in the driveway. It didn't matter, we left anyway. Bill drove up to the bedroom doors. I was glad, because this way we wouldn't have to walk directly past James. I tried the odd shaped, antique-looking key that I had found earlier in the afternoon. It fit! Bill carried the two suitcases. At that moment I had no idea what was in them. Melissa hurried back into the house to grab our pillows. Susan rescued sleeping Nekessa, and I loaded Otiga into a blanket and hurried out with him.

James was heading our way. I whispered to Susan, "Tell him we are taking Otiga to Nairobi because he is sick." I don't know if he believed this but he stopped coming towards us. He didn't try to stop us from leaving! We had made it out of the house. It was just a few minutes to our meeting point with Dan. This was also where we were taking Susan. I knew she would be with a caring family, but it was so painful leaving her. This was too much fear and sorrow for her to face alone! I loved her so much, and I knew she loved us. "Susan, I want you to explain to Peter and Juliet why we had to go, and why I couldn't say good-bye. Please tell them I love them, and I will always love all of you." There was no time for long good-byes. Maybe that was best. My heart was so tired of breaking.

The men transferred the suitcases while Missy and I carried the little ones. I waved to Susan as we drove away. I would never see her again.

As we left the Blind School, I overheard Dan talking to Bill. "The flight has been moved up an hour. The plane is now leaving at 11:00 PM. It's still possible to make it to the airport if everything goes smoothly, but it's going to be close."

"What about the three police checks along this road?" Bill asked. "If we're stopped at any one of them, we'll miss the flight." I thought about what he was saying. It was very unusual not to be stopped at least once, and it was possible to be pulled over for a police check at all three locations! If they noticed our anxiety, they might even detain us for questioning.

We had come too far to have it fail now. I thought of all the obstacles that had been overcome. I let go of this concern and concentrated on my three children. They hadn't had three days to emotionally prepare for this trip, and they were awakened from a peaceful sleep only to be thrown into fear and uncertainty. Kessy was doing the best, but she was too little to understand. Otiga had heard his name mentioned and began asking questions. "Mommy, where are we going? Am I really sick? Are you taking me to the hospital?"

I held him closer as Melissa joined in with more questions. She was old enough to understand the seriousness of the situation. She looked at me and asked in a trembling voice, "Will we be safe? Are we going to America now?"

The words, "Are we going to America?" echoed from Otiga, as he started to squirm in my arms with excitement. I gave them my bravest voice, "We'll be fine, Melissa. Otiga, you're not going to the hospital. We're all going to get on a plane and fly to America to see Grandma and Grandpa."

Dan was very quiet. This was strange. Was there something he hadn't told me? I didn't want to ask; I had enough to think about. I began taking a mental inventory of the last half-hour. I had no idea what I had packed, Other than some pictures and the pillows Melissa had grabbed at the last moment. This brought a smile to my mind. Pillows! We were carrying pillows in a suitcase! I looked over the children. I had forgotten to get shoes for both Otiga and Nekessa. How could I have missed shoes! Maybe it was because they rarely wore them in Kenya.

Dan's voice brought me back from my thoughts. He was ready to share the reason for his silence. He handed me Otiga's and Nekessa's passports to look over. "Notice the date," he said. "They are dated March 9, 1982. Now look at Melissa's passport. It's dated October 11, 1980." He quietly added, "The authorities may have some questions with this difference, and with the fact that two of the passports are dated with today's date. If they suspect anything they could hold us and contact Otieno." There was no way to avoid the authorities. We had to go through their security check. Dan continued to talk, "I'll call your parents as soon as you're in the air. Now, let's go over the last minute details before we arrive at the airport."

It was difficult concentrating on what he was saying. These were my last remaining minutes in Kenya. I was scared. Passing through security could be dangerous. What if I appeared suspicious? We could be arrested on the spot!

What if my family didn't want us to come home? It had been almost two years since we had left America. I was melancholy about leaving Kenya, and yet we must leave. I knew that with my mind, but my heart was deaf to the facts. We had given up everything to come to Kenya. It was Otieno's dream, but I had adopted it as mine, also. Now the dream had turned into a nightmare.

We pulled into the airport just minutes before it was time to board. The three police check points between Thika and Nairobi rushed into my thoughts. We hadn't been stopped at any of them. If we had been, we would definitely have missed the plane! I was quivering inside as we approached the customs officer. "Please don't let it show on the outside," I prayed silently. As if he understood, Dan took the lead, and began talking. This was probably best, because I was beginning to quiver on the outside, also. He spoke calmly but quickly, "May I have permission to help them carry their luggage back to the plane? She has too much to carry herself." They agreed without asking any question! This was amazing! They told us to hurry, as they rushed us past their post, barely noticing our official papers. They were concerned that we not delay because the last boarding call had been given. Obsessed with our need to move quickly, they seemed blind to the unusual nature of our papers.

Once again I stood in amazement as the impossible became possible, and then it was suddenly clear. There had been no reason to be concerned. This entire operation was in God's Hands. Who else could have caused so many "coincidences" to happen? From that moment on Saturday evening, when I was lying on the cement at the Country Club, and I realized what I must do, God had been in control of all the details. Miracles did still happen, and we were living one! The same thought must have come to Dan, because when I looked at him a similar confident smile was on his face. They allowed Dan to carry Otiga onto the plane for me, while I carried Nekessa. We had found a pair of shoes in Dan's car that almost fit Otiga, but Nekessa was still barefoot. As Dan turned to leave he handed me an envelope and said, "You're not to open this until the plane has taken off."

What could I say to him at a moment like this? He and Cathy had been more than "just friends." They had helped give us our freedom, while they had taken a chance of losing theirs. This family gave their love, money, and time, knowing we had nothing to give back to them. There were no words meaningful enough to say in the few seconds we had remaining. He gently hugged Otiga, Nekessa, Melissa, and me, then turned and walked down the isle of the plane. This episode was not yet over for the Schellenbergs because tomorrow they would be faced head-on with Otieno's wrath. The force of the plane pushed against our bodies as it began to increase in speed, and we were gently lifted into the air. Tears filled my heart and eyes. They were tears of relief, joy, and sorrow. I knew our episode wasn't over yet either, but I had learned an important lesson.

God had lifted us out of Africa in a miraculous way, and He wouldn't just drop us somewhere, forgotten. No matter how difficult the challenge, I knew we would not have to face it alone.

# CHAPTER 12: DADDY MAY WE PLEASE COME HOME

## *So Much Forgiveness*

As the plane climbed higher, my spirit soared! We had escaped, and we were on our way home. It had seemed impossible, but we were high above Kenya, and safe from the fears that lingered below. It would have been easy to dwell on these thoughts but it was time to look forward. Our first stop would be Holland. We would then fly to New York, change airlines, and our next stop would be home. "Home," the word brought so many mixed feelings to my heart. I wondered if Dan had called my parents yet, and how they would accept the news.

Dan! That reminded me of the envelope he handed me just before he left the plane. I quickly opened it, and inside was a card that Cathy had painted the last day we were together. A calm feeling came over me, as I looked at the delicate little bird on the card. It reminded me of the times I had spent with Cathy, quiet peaceful times that had renewed my strength. Inside the card was a note.

Dear Carole,

You watched me paint this one, so I hope you will like it. Happy Birthday. I would have waited. I will miss you like a sister. No, more, because I don't know when we will meet again. We love you, and it's been to our advantage to have met you and helped you. Don't cry anymore.

The Lord loves you as you are.
Cathy
P.S. This $200 is your early birthday present.

Tucked safely within the card were two $100 bills. They had thought of everything! They knew I had no American money, actually no money of any kind. It was Tuesday night, and we wouldn't be landing in Columbus, Ohio, until late Wednesday night, almost twenty-four hours later. We would need this money. We had a six-hour layover in Holland.

## THE REST OF THE STORY ~

Otiga and Nekessa were asleep on blankets on the floor in front of my seat. The gentleman sitting ahead of us had suggested that this was the safest and most comfortable place for them. I knew they couldn't possibly understand all that had happened. I wasn't sure I did. They were too small to comprehend the life we had just ended, or the life we were about to begin.

Melissa was older, and she vaguely knew why we must leave. She was also in tune with the uncertainties we were facing. Her questions echoed again and again in my head, "Mommy, we have no money, no car, and no job. How will we live? We have no house. Will Otieno come after us? Will Grandpa be happy we are coming home?"

I couldn't answer her questions; I couldn't even think about them at this moment. It was not time to face survival questions. We just needed to make this journey home.

I smiled at Missy and answered her with all the courage I had. "Dear, God will take care of us tomorrow, just as He has taken care of us tonight." I thought about my answer, and it comforted me, also.

Holland was much colder than Kenya had been. As we left the plane, I realized we needed coats. Kessy was shoeless, so I carried her from the plane and through customs. I don't remember how I selected a hotel, but we arrived there by bus. The first thing I did after we were taken to our room was bathe the children. Then I bathed. Not an everyday bath that merely consists of becoming clean and refreshed. I was determined to wash off the red dust of Thika. I wanted to rid myself of the dust in my mind that kept clouding my thoughts, the dust that was causing my eyes to cry, and the deep, down-in dust that had entered my heart and was causing it to break. I was determined to wash away the painful memories and the fears. But I wasn't successful. I should have known better than to think it would be this easy. It would take time, much time.

We must have been a sad sight that morning in Holland. It was around 11:00 A.M. We were obviously very clean, but must have appeared helpless or homeless as we wandered through the hotel, looking for a restaurant. Unfortunately they had just closed after breakfast, and they wouldn't be opening again for an hour or so. I was carrying my little shoeless Kessy, and holding Otiga's hand. Melissa was close beside me. I asked a waiter if he knew of any restaurants that were open. He looked at us for a moment, and then spoke to us in English, "Follow me." We went past a sign in front of the restaurant that read, "Closed until 12:30 P.M." He led us to the cocktail bar, and told us to sit down on the barstools. He disappeared for a few minutes, and when he returned, he had cheese sandwiches and Cokes for all of us. I thanked him, and asked how much I owed him. He smiled and said, "It costs nothing, just enjoy it." I was grateful, but somewhat embarrassed. It made me realize how pathetic we looked with no shoes on Kessy and no coats on any of us in this cold March weather in Holland.

It was nearly time to return to the airport. As we rode along in the clean, comfortable bus, I was captured by the beauty all around us. Under Other circumstances it would have been nice to linger awhile in this picturesque country, but not today. Today we were going home; and like homing pigeons, nothing could change our course. We boarded the plane as soon as it was possible. In a few hours we would be in New York. I was determined to kiss the ground when we arrived.

Unfortunately, I was unable to do this because I was too busy with my sweet Melissa. On our flight from Holland to New York, she became very ill, and spent much of the time in the bathroom. She tried hard to be brave, but she lost everything including her bravery in the bathroom. She was weak and drained.

My heart sank into my stomach for her. Since Melissa couldn't leave the restroom, we were unable to leave the plane when it landed. All the Other passengers had left, and the cleaning crew was preparing for the next flight. When she finally was able to come out of the bathroom, she was very pale

Since we were so late departing from the plane, the airline apparently had assigned a man to escort us. He took Nekessa from my arms, and then gently lifted up Otiga. He was one of the largest men I had ever seen! Otiga and Nekessa looked like little dolls in his huge arms. He led us through hallways and locked doors until we exited somewhere in the New York airport. He took us through customs and then transferred our luggage and obtained our boarding passes. Finally, he took us to the departing bus area and waited with us until the bus arrived. As he carried the children onto the bus, he spoke directly to the driver, "This family is going to the Pan Am terminal. Would you take special care to see that they arrive there?" He smiled at us as he took back his coat that he had wrapped around the little ones.

I couldn't believe what had just happened. Did things like this really occur in New York? Was this gentle giant a guardian angel? He looked real, except for his larger-than-life size and his larger-than-life heart. Once again I had worried for nothing. When would I learn?

I didn't have time to kiss the ground when we arrived in America, so I kissed Melissa as we flew out of New York. She had gone through a very difficult time, but she seemed to be regaining her color.

It was dark as we flew towards Columbus, Ohio. All the children were asleep now. It had been a long tiring trip. They had come halfway around the world, and that was enough excitement for one day. I was glad they were sleeping. It gave me time to prepare for our arrival. I went to the restroom to freshen up. As I looked into the mirror, I stared at a thirty-six-year-old woman, but tonight I looked older. The stress was showing on my face, and makeup didn't help.

I thought about my parents. My father and mother had done everything they could to convince me not to marry Otieno, but I wouldn't listen. I knew I would have to swallow my pride and accept their, "I told you so!" I could do this; I was broken, and very humble.

The stewardess announced, "We will be landing soon. Everyone must return to your seat, and fasten your seat belt." Every muscle in my body began to tense! In a few minutes we would be landing. Would my parents be waiting for us? Would they be happy about our returning? I would need their support, both financially and emotionally, because I was bankrupt in both areas.

I awakened the children, and told them we were home. Melissa was excited, Otiga vaguely remembered his grandparents, and although Nekessa had no memories, she was willing to share in my excitement. We exited the plane, and began the long walk through the hallway leading into the Columbus Airport.

I should have been running, but I held back. Then I saw him... my father. He was standing at the opening of the hallway. He looked frantic! His eyes were half closed as he squinted to see into the dimly lit passageway. I could feel his fear. I looked into his eyes, as he found us. I felt his love, and I saw his relief, as he realized we were almost within his reach.

He didn't hug us separately; he held all four of us tightly in his arms, rocking us gently. There was no, "I told you so," only, "I love you so."

It was over. We were home, and we were safe. There would be a time when I would share why we had to leave Kenya, but not now. Tonight, we would just share the joy of being together.

# CHAPTER 13: A NEW SONG TO SING

## *So Many Blessings*

**July, 1982**: I rolled over on my stomach and shielded my eyes from the glaring sun reflecting off the cement. A quick inventory of the small heads bobbing around in the pool brought Otiga and Nekessa into focus. Finding them was easy. They were the only small brown bodies with iridescent orange floatation devices on their arms. I watched my little fish playing in the pool. They had adjusted well to their new home, probably better than I had. They weren't plagued by the fears of the past and the uncertainties of the future.

I still cried sometimes, but not as often as I had when we first arrived. I still avoided people occasionally, when I didn't feel comfortable talking about the past two years in Africa. I enjoyed sharing the slow paced culture of Thika, the magnificent sunsets, and the endearing people who welcomed us with unconditional love and acceptance. Sharing that I had to escape one night with only my three children, two suitcases, and a broken heart, brought back the sadness and shame.

My mind was yanked back into the present by the sight of the mailman. Pulling my water-soaked, raisin-skinned children from the pool, I eagerly followed him. They left a trail of tiny puddles as their footsteps deposited the water that ran down their legs. Maybe today I'd receive a job offer from one of the schools, not just a polite rejection letter. Living a life of leisure was fun, but I was ready to move on.

"I'll give you my first-born child, if you have a job offer for me today,"

I teased, as I caught up with the mailman. He was accustomed to this urgency in my voice. His downcast expression and empty hands said all that needed to be said. He walked on to the next house. Gathering Nekessa in my arms, I herded Otiga toward our apartment. Melissa, Otiga, Nekessa, and I had been home from Kenya since March. It was now July. We were living in an apartment my parents had rented for us when we returned. They had left Florida to help us get settled in Ohio, and they were returning to Florida in November. I had applied to every school system, both public and private. There were no teaching positions available in Columbus, Ohio. A friend of mine who worked in the administration office told me they were letting teachers go, not hiring them.

After returning to America, it had been therapeutic to have the time to rest and re-group, but this R&R had lasted long enough. I was ready to become a productive part of our capitalistic society. Why couldn't I find work? Maybe I needed to branch out, forget teaching. I checked the job offers in the Columbus newspaper. Within one week I was interviewing for a position as an inner-city counselor. They wanted me! It sounded interesting. I'd be working in a neighborhood program that helped kids find productive ways to spend their free time. Since the program was geared towards after-school and Saturdays, I'd be working evenings and weekends. The challenge excited me; and I loved working with children. This unstructured program would give me free rein to implement ideas of my own. However, lurking underneath the excitement of this job were too many red flags about the hours. I would have to leave my children two evenings a week and Saturdays. This would not be good for them.

They had been through enough anxiety in the past few months. Melissa was a strong natural leader and a loving care giver for her brother and sister. However, she would soon be attending school, and she didn't need any extra responsibility. Otiga was the "super-ball" of the three. He had bounced back quickly from the sudden uprooting and re-planting. He appeared to have the inner strength and outer charisma needed to deal with the stress he had been through. Then again, it may have been that he was just a normal five year old boy who loved to play, and didn't have any time or interest to think about the past. Kessy seemed to internalize her feelings and let them mushroom within. She had almost stopped talking when we first arrived; but she was gradually coming out of the trauma. I knew that taking this job was wrong, but I needed a job!

That evening, as I shared the job offer with my father, I could see that he didn't like the idea either. Whenever he was worried, he would squint his eyebrows together. He poured a glass of milk as he spoke, "This isn't the right job, Carole."

"It's the only offer I've had, Dad," I argued. "I can't go on forever letting you pay my bills. It's been four months, and nothing has opened up." I tossed the growing mound of polite rejection letters in front of him.

Dad's eyebrows grew close again. "Carole, your mother and I don't want you to remain in Ohio. We want you to move to Florida so you won't be so far from us. Consider this idea. Fly to Florida and stay with your brother for one week. We'll keep the children while you're gone. During that time, apply for a teaching position. If there's an opening, move to Florida. We'll help you financially until you're settled." His eyebrows almost became one, "Don't stay here, Carole. We've spent two years in fear while you were in Africa. We don't want to worry long distance anymore."

I understood his words, and the stress in his voice. I had put them through enough grief already. I would honor their request. Besides, without them and my two brothers, Ohio would no longer be home.

The trip to Orlando was a good decision. I hadn't seen my brother, Fred, in two years. While I was in Kenya, he was married, and now he and his wife Diane had a two-month-old baby girl. I was glad I had agreed to spend a week with them. I really didn't believe the job market would be any different there, but it was the perfect opportunity to spend time with my brother and his family.

I had time to think and pray during the flight. I thought about the job offer in Columbus, and how wrong it was for our family. I didn't need a job. I needed the right job for my children and me. Maybe Orlando held the answer.

I left an unusually humid July day in Ohio, and had stepped out into an unusually balmy evening in Orlando. The trip was looking better. In Kenya I had discovered I was like a hothouse plant, thriving in warm weather. Orlando had definite potential. I searched the faces of the people searching our faces. No eyes connected. Then I saw my brother standing in the distance, holding a small, blanketed being.

The reunion was joyous! Tears flowed freely. No one listened as everyone talked. "I had nightmares that I'd never see you again." My brother's quivering voice choked up as he spoke.

"So did I," I answered as I held his baby girl in my arms for the first time.

Intimate gatherings of palm trees, and glistening lakes paraded before us on our trip to his home. I liked it here, but I couldn't be bought easily. I had witnessed exquisite beauty in Kenya. I had a mission to accomplish, and I must not be sidetracked from my purpose.

The following morning I began mapping out interviews that I had set up while I was in Ohio. I had almost every day filled, and Fred had also scheduled some appointments for me. I felt strangely encouraged as I set out on my safari to capture a job. I spent my days being professional, and my nights being silly with my baby brother and his wife. We even had some time to be serious, something we seldom did together.

I shared with him my feelings about my hope for the future. Psalm 40 stated it best, "I waited patiently for the Lord; He turned to me and heard my cry. He lifted me out of the miry pit, out of the mud and mire; He set my feet on a rock and gave me a firm place to stand. He put a new song in my mouth, a hymn of praise to our God…"

When we escaped from Kenya it was as though God had heard my cry and lifted us out of our pit of despair. When we arrived in America our feet were set on steady ground. Possibly, my trip to Orlando was the beginning of a new song in my heart. God had a plan, and maybe

His plan would be revealed in this enjoyable city where Mickey Mouse lived.

On Monday morning, I found my way to the office of the Orange County School system. The interview was uneventful. If there were any openings, a principal from a specific school would contact me. It didn't sound promising, but there were other possibilities still pending. Tuesday morning was even less encouraging. When I called to confirm a previously scheduled appointment in Ocala, the secretary was in no mood to talk. The principal had just been rushed to the hospital.

I no longer had the interview for today, so I adjusted my tempo to a slower pace and poured myself a second cup of coffee. I needed a new plan. I was in Florida to look for a teaching position; so I decided to let "my fingers do the walking" through the private school listings in the Yellow Pages. Mind-boggling! There were too many private schools to consider!

Before I tossed the phone book down, my eyes fell upon the listing for Edgewood Children's Ranch. I called this number and no others. The receptionist connected me with Dr. Lynd, the Director of the Ranch. He asked me the usual questions and we discovered we were both Buckeyes, natives of Ohio. I enjoyed the easy, flowing conversation. It didn't feel like business. His next words totally amazed me. "Last Friday, one of our teachers, decided to return to Ohio and enter the seminary. We have been praying that the Lord would send the right teacher to us."

I agreed to an interview and a tour on Friday, the only day that I had open. My heartbeat quickened from our discussion. I knew it was not a coincidence that I had chosen only this private school to call, and that they had been praying for a teacher. I thought of the Ranch often during the rest of the week.

I had spent six years of my early childhood in a similar environment because my parents had been the directors of the children's home in Marion Ohio. We had moved to the children's home when I was just five years old, and my most vivid childhood memories were of this period

115

of my life. I laughed when I thought of the question Melissa had asked one evening while we were all talking at the dinner table, "Mom, why can't we live somewhere like you did when you were a kid." My children loved stories about the children's home, especially when Mom, Dad, and I began "remembering when." It would not be difficult for me to re-enter that type of environment with my children. They would probably feel comfortable because of the stories they had happily absorbed from the memories of my childhood.

The week passed quickly. It was already Friday, and I was getting homesick for my children. This would be my last interview. I would be leaving on Sunday. I called my parents to see how the little ones were doing. Dad answered, "They hardly realize you're gone." I told him about the Ranch. His response was excited, "If you like the Ranch, call me back, and we'll discuss the salary and benefits. We can drive the children down later, if you decide to stay. Keep me informed."

The Ranch was about a thirty-minute drive from my brother's house, and not easy to find. As I drove, I had serious doubts I'd ever locate it. After driving between armies of orange trees, standing in formation on either side of the narrow country road, I came upon a quaint, hand painted sign that read, "Edgewood Ranch, Invest in a Child's Eternity." I drove down the long entrance that was framed by neat rows of orange trees. There were white stucco cottages arranged in a semi-circle around the blue and white main office building. Children in red and white checked shirts added splotches of color to the landscape. It seemed as if the land went on forever. A baseball diamond, a track, and a football field broke up the greenness. Just beyond a hill was a sandy beach that led into a crystal clear blue lake.

I parked the car and began walking towards the office. There was something wrong here! I had been at interviews all week. Each time before, I had felt anxious as I approached the office. I didn't feel uneasy this time, but I did feel something very strongly. As I walked past the rose garden, so full of roses that they seemed to reach out and beg to be touched, I understood what it was. I felt as if I was home. How could this be? I had never been here before, but that was what I was experiencing. Deep inside me was a calmness that reached out to touch the outermost parts of my body.

The interview didn't dissolve this peace. Dr. Lynd, the Director, explained the purpose and procedures of the Ranch. It was a non-denominational, Christian residential center for children. The Ranch was operated on faith, and no denomination was solely responsible for the support of this program. The parents paid according to their ability to pay. All the food was donated. "Sometimes," he said, "the pay checks are a little late."

We walked across campus to meet Dr. Joan Consolver, the school administrator. We sat down to talk and I felt so at ease with this stranger that I forgot she was a stranger. After reviewing my resume and the typical job interview questions, she asked, "Why did you leave Kenya?" The question hit me off guard and I felt tears burning my eyes.

"My husband and I were married six years ago in America. When we moved to Kenya, he didn't tell me that one of my duties as his wife was to be beaten when he chose to do this to me." I stopped talking for a moment to breathe again.

"I knew I had to leave, but I didn't know how. He had taken the children's passports and I couldn't even leave Kenya without his permission. My best friends, missionaries from America, organized our escape. It was truly a miracle.

Joanie listened without commenting. When I finished, she spoke with compassion and concern. "We need you here, and you and your children need to be here." She prayed with me, and then sent me back to finish the interview with Dr. Lynd.

When I arrived, Dr. Lynd had the paperwork ready, and he began talking, "Carole, I'd like you to start on Monday. The students have already arrived on campus. It will take about two weeks for your training." Then he shared that housing on grounds and health insurance would be included with the teaching position that he was offering me.

The questions that Melissa had asked me as we were flying home to America came back to me. "How are we going to live, Mommy? We have no house, no money, no car, and you have no job." At that time, I had no answers.

Each question that Melissa had asked was being answered now. Every detail was included in this unbelievable offer. It was as though this position and all its benefits were created just to meet our needs! I would receive a salary, housing on the Ranch, and insurance.

I would not have to worry about the children being alone when they returned home from school. I wouldn't be working on evenings or weekends. We'd be living in a loving, sheltered environment. I didn't have a car yet, but I wouldn't need one right away because I could walk to work.

Before I answered him, I thought about my plan. I was not going to accept any job offer without discussing it first with my father. The words, "My Father," echoed in my mind. I had spoken to my Heavenly Father, and He had answered me. He had provided for our every need with this job offer. It wasn't just a good job for me; it was an excellent environment for my family. That's why I had felt at home when I walked across the grounds earlier. God was quietly telling me that this was where He wanted us to be. Before I could answer him, Dr. Lynd's wife came into the office, carrying a dozen yellow roses. There was every color of rose in that garden, but she had unknowingly selected my favorite.

"Yes, I would like to begin on Monday," I answered. I knew the children would be safe with my parents until they could join me. I had nothing to move, I had left it all in Kenya. As I drove to my brother's house that afternoon, a song sung by The Bill Gaither Trio floated into my memory:

**"Something Beautiful, Something good,
All my confusion, He understood.
All I had to offer Him was brokenness and strife;
But He made something beautiful of my life."**

God had given me His plan. He had shown me where we were to be planted. Here, I could grow stronger emotionally, physically, and spiritually; and I could vaccinate my children with this strength. I had rested in Ohio. Now it was time to make a new life for my children and myself. I could use the tough times we'd been through to relate to the children who came to the Ranch broken and afraid. I knew the journey back wouldn't be easy; I'd left so much of me in Kenya.

I was not to come here to hide from the world. I was to use my gifts to help broken children heal. Jesus would take the brokenness and confusion of my life, and turn it into something beautiful here at Edgewood Children's Ranch. I had a New Song to Sing. It was time to sing it joyfully.

### Psalm 40: 1-3, 5

I waited patiently for the Lord;
He turned to me and heard my cry.
He lifted me out of the slimy pit,
Out of the mud and mire;
He set my feet on a rock
and gave me a firm place to stand.
He put a new song in my mouth,
a hymn of praise to our God.
Many will see and fear
and put their trust in the Lord.
Many, O Lord my God,
are the wonders you have done.
The things you planned for us
no one can recount to you;
Were I to speak and tell of them,
they would be too many to declare.

### New International Version

# Author's Update
## 2012

It has been 30 years since the children and I returned to America. My story began pushing its way out of my heart and onto a notebook as I was flying from Ohio to Florida, four months after we arrived home. God has been our strength and our peace as He has cared for us throughout these years.

Nekessa was only three when we returned. She was the most traumatized at the time. She actually stopped talking for awhile. However, she has grown into a confident, strong woman who quietly shares her blessings with others who may need a little help. Nekessa graduated from the University of Florida and then received her Masters of Science at Ohio State University. She also met her husband Boon at OSU. She is now a Nurse Practioner in Women's health and Boon is a Nurse Practioner in Cardiology. They have two beautiful daughters.

Otiga was five years old when we returned, and he was full of charm. He had a rollercoaster life as he was becoming the young man he is today. Otiga is now married, and he and his wife, Andrea, are both in college and they have a five year old son, Octavius, who is also full of life and charm. Neither Otiga nor Octavius has ever met a stranger. My loving father died in 1994, but his gregarious personality lives on in both Otiga and Octavius.

Melissa was ten when we returned. She graduated from Miami University (OH), where she met her husband. They have two spunky children who love sports and school. Melissa has never been afraid to stretch her boundaries and tackle a challenge. Her strength of character, love of family, and anyone else in need of love, shines throughout everything she does.

After I began teaching at Edgewood Children's Ranch, God gave me an interesting gift wrapped in a tree. His name was Bruce and he was trimming a branch next to my house. He also worked at Edgewood. I didn't think I needed a Bruce in my life, but he lovingly helped heal the wounds in my heart. We were married eight years later, and we have been married for twenty-two years. He is the most gentle, caring man I have ever known. God must smile at us because Bruce and I both know that we are His special gift to each Other.

Keeping in touch with Susan, Peter and Juliet was very difficult. I heard from the Schellenbergs that Susan returned to our house a few days after we left Kenya. She wanted to be with Peter and Juliet. However, Otieno sent her back to the village. She eventually married, and has remained on the island.

Peter and Juliet remained with Otieno in Thika, and they both continued school. When Juliet was just a teen, she died from aids. I didn't hear about it until long after she was gone. Peter finished his education and was planning to become a pastor, but instead he returned to the island to be a fisherman. Sometime in his early twenties he also died from aids. I have felt such sadness for Peter and Juliet throughout the years. I wish I knew that there had been someone to love and comfort them during this terrifying death. However, I'm afraid that too many people were facing the same suffering at that time, and there may not have been enough care to go around.

I know that Peter and Juliet understood the love of Jesus while we were together, and they loved Him. I have to believe that Jesus was their comforter during this agonizing time, and that we will be together again in Heaven.

Grandma Auma passed away a few years after we left Thika. It was her dream to be buried in her special ceremonial dress, scarf, and earrings that the children and I gave her on Christmas day. I hope that she got her wish! I know that she will also be part of our celebration in Heaven.

The day after we left, Otieno moved another woman into our house. However, he wrote an interesting letter to my father thanking him for taking care of us until we returned to Africa. Nothing in the letter even suggested that there had been any problems. He told my dad that I knew we were meant to be together. During the first year that we were home, he sent a few letters proclaiming his sorrow that we were gone, and then asking if I would please send him a supply of Captain Black tobacco, or an engine for his fishing boat on the island. After Otiga and Nekessa were grown, they would attempt to write Otieno. He occasionally wrote back. I never discouraged them from reaching out to their father. They needed that connection and I wanted them to be proud of their African heritage.

Otieno retired from Del Monte about eleven years ago. He said he was returning to Sigulu Island to live. Through the miracle of the internet, Otiga has discovered that he and Nekessa have about sixteen brothers and sisters. One was actually studying at a university in VA. They knew who Otiga was because Otieno talked about him throughout the years.

After Dan and Cathy Schellenberg helped us escape, they had to remain in Thika and face whatever repercussions might arise. They took their four children and left Thika for a few days just to be on the safe side. Otieno never tried to say or do anything to them. However, months later, James, our guard, approached Dan. He wanted him to know that he had recognized the man who had helped us escape. Then he added with a smile that he also knew what we were doing that night, and he let us go because he knew that Otieno was treating me badly. He covered himself by telling him that he had been drinking that night and had fallen asleep on the job.

The Schellenbergs returned to America several years later. They are living and working in Texas. Dan has written an amazing book, *Under the Talking Tree, a Guide to African Semi-Arid Homestead Self-Reliance.* He and Cathy have built their own home using the principles in his book. His masterpiece addresses today's urgent need for living a self reliant life and reducing our dependency on fossil fuel. Cathy is a talented artist, a nurse, mother and grandmother. They will remain forever in my heart as living examples of God's love.

# EPILOGUE 2010

## *The Circle of Life*

The day was almost here; July 17, 2010; Andrea and Otiga's wedding day. Melissa, now thirty-eight, Otiga, thirty-three, and Nekessa, thirty-one, and I had been imagining, and critiquing this event since Nekessa's earth-shaking proposal that reached across to the other side of the planet. Her wedding present to Otiga was to give him his life long dream to see his father, Otieno Habembe. Actually, it had been her dream also. When she received her master's degree from Ohio State University, she offered to fly Otieno from Kenya to Ohio, so that he could attend her graduation. He interpreted this invitation as an opportunity for Kessy to also pay for one of his children to come with him so she withdrew her offer. The wedding was her last attempt at making this dream come true.

During the month before the wedding, Kessy, Otiga, Melissa, and I discussed or e-mailed every fact or fictional possibility that our memories or imagination could conger up about Otieno. I don't know what we accomplished, but our emotions ran deep as we tried to fit together the pieces of the puzzle that became an uncanny journey back in time.

Thirty years ago, in July of 1980, Otieno, Otiga and Nekessa left our home in Fort Wayne, Indiana and flew to our new home in Thika, Kenya. Melissa and I followed two and a half months later. How ironic it was that Otiga had fallen in love with Andrea, a beautiful young woman who lived in Fort Wayne, Indiana, and in July, 2010, Otieno was returning to Fort Wayne from Kenya to attend their wedding.

It was Thursday, July 15, just two days before the wedding as Bruce and I boarded the plane in Orlando to join the rest of our family and friends in Fort Wayne, Indiana. There were so many thoughts, both lovely and painful, revisiting my mind as we sped toward our destination. Thirty years felt like only 10 years, but Melissa, Nekessa and Otiga now had beautiful children of their own.

Melissa and Nekessa seemed to flow smoothly through the trials of their teenage years. The challenging times centered on Otiga. I was told that his name, Habembe, meant warrior, and during his late teens and early twenties, he was often at war with himself. Otiga easily achieved everything he attempted; sports, leadership positions, professional acting, and lucrative job opportunities. He would accomplish his goal and then self-destruct. His major tools of destruction were alcohol and his refusal to surrender to God.

He dabbled in college, but the sweetness of large paychecks, as he was succeeding in business, diminished the importance of furthering his education. In 2004, when Otiga met Andrea, the battle of self-destruction was raging within him. It is not easy to remain charming when you are trying to hide a drinking problem. It was even more difficult when Andrea became pregnant. They were living in Orlando at that time and she was far away from her home and her parents. She didn't know Jesus, and she didn't know she needed to, until all of this became more than she could bear. It was a frightening time for Andrea, but it was the perfect time for her to hear about Jesus and to experience His unconditional love, as our family also loved her unconditionally. Melissa and Nekessa were wonderful encouragers as the baby grew inside of Andrea.

Unfortunately, Otiga wasn't always the man Andrea needed him to be, because he was fighting his own demons. During this challenging time, Andrea surrendered her life and her fears to Jesus. The transformation was beautiful. She had a peace within her, when there was no reason for her to be at peace. As the baby grew, Andrea was growing into an exceptional mother.

When Octavius was a few months old, the company moved Otiga back to the Midwest, and they returned to Fort Wayne, Indiana. Her parents were delighted that she was home. Andrea was only twenty, but she had grown wise beyond her years. She began attending Pine Hills Church, where she was embraced by a women's group that offered her not only Godly advice but also love and support.

As Andrea grew closer to God, Otiga slipped further into alcohol, but she never gave up on him. Late one night in early November, 2007, Andrea called me. Otiga was unconscious and had been taken to the hospital. He was in intensive care because his organs were shutting down. Otiga had given up on his body and now his body was giving up on him. For three weeks, I watched a team of doctor's work to save my son's life. There were many people praying for him, but there had been so many people praying for Otiga for a long time.

On Saturday, a week before Thanksgiving, Otiga and I were watching the FL. Gators game in his hospital room. During a close-up of Tim Teboe's face, he saw a Bible verse written in black under his eyes; *Philippians 4:13*. Otiga wrote it down; "I can do all things through Christ who strengthens me."

That night when I went back to his apartment, Otiga called to tell me about a bottle of vodka that was hidden under his mattress, and he asked me to pour it out. Otiga was released from the hospital a few days later, but more important than that, he had surrendered his life to God, and God had released him from his addiction to alcohol The tools of Otiga's destruction were shattered in one moment of total surrender God had a plan for my son, and it was for good, not evil. As the weeks and months melted into a year, I understood why Andrea had not given up on Otiga. God's plan was for them to be together as Godly parents for Octavius. Pine Hills, the church that had embraced Andrea, now opened their arms and their hearts to Otiga. Mike Drury, the pastor of the church, spent many months counseling them. They were eager students, and now in just two days the celebration of God's love for them and their love for Him and for each Other would take place at the Pine Hills Church in Fort Wayne. The trip this weekend was going to encompass so much more than the wedding for our family. Everyone understood this, but no one knew what to expect.

Otieno had flown into North Carolina on July, 11th to be with Nekessa, her husband Boon, and their two year old daughter. Nekessa had planned every detail of how she would meet her father at the airport. Kessy wanted to pick him up by herself so that no one would interfere with their reunion. This was a very important moment for her. She wanted to have time to be with her father before the wedding. As a special gift to Otieno, she was driving him to Columbus, Ohio, so he could visit Ohio State, his alma mater.

Their meeting was nothing like Kessy had imagined. She wanted to hear his memories of the things they had done together in Kenya. He wanted to hear all about Otiga and talk about Otiga. She wanted to create new memories while they were together now. He wanted Nekessa to buy him Captain Black tobacco. He wanted her to buy him a new pipe for the tobacco. He wanted her to buy dresses to take home to his wives and other women who lived on the island. He wanted her to buy new clothes for him.

He wanted her to plan a meeting with his college roommate who lived in Indiana. He seemed to have forgotten that she had arranged and financed his entire trip to America. He treated her as if she was his daughter in Kenya, and in Kenya, daughters can never be as valuable as sons. However, Kessy did quite well with her father. She saw Otieno as he was, not as how she dreamed he would be..

Otiga had no expectations of his father. He considered him his sperm donor. Bruce was his father, and Otiga would not share that title with Otieno. However, he included him in all the wedding activities. Otiga took him around Fort Wayne to see everything he asked to visit. He allowed Otieno to give a speech that he had prepared for the wedding reception.

I found it truly amazing to watch Otiga and Otieno together. They walked alike, they moved alike, they even rubbed their heads in the same way when they were thinking. Otieno's smile had been cut and pasted onto Otiga's face.

Kessy had only one request for me when I arrived in Fort Wayne. She wanted me to stand next to Otieno so that she could see her mother and father together. She had talked about this from the moment she had scheduled his flight. It was the little girl in her that needed this picture for her memory bank.

Melissa didn't have any expectations. She was 10 yrs old when we left Africa, so she remembered Otieno. Her concerns were for Kessy, Otiga and me, and she did not want Otieno to interfere in any way with the beauty and the ambiance of the wedding.

I had mixed emotions, but I wasn't excited or afraid. The feelings were more subdued, like faded black and white pictures. I remembered the passion and the excitement, then the disenchantment, the pain, and the fear, but I didn't feel any of those emotions now. I wanted to face Otieno and ask why? The thoughts in my mind were loud and clear. I wanted him to see his children and grandchildren, and to recognize how remarkable they were, and to shower them with love and praise.

It was a balmy afternoon when Bruce and I arrived at the apartment complex where Melissa and Nekessa's families were staying. It was the perfect housing arrangement. Each family had a furnished apartment within the same building. Otieno was staying with Nekessa and her family.

Everyone was outside talking and enjoying the weather when Otiga returned from the airport with Bruce and me. The girls and the grandchildren welcomed us with hugs and kisses, and then as the grandchildren ran off to play, Kessy took my hand and escorted me over to her father. I felt awkward as he came closer. The last time I had been with him, he had knocked me to the ground. Now we were standing face to face and he was smiling at me. Kessy saved this moment as she quickly took our picture. She was content. She had a photo of her mother and father standing together.

I didn't get to tell Otieno the things I wanted him to know, and I didn't get to ask him the questions I wanted to ask. I wasn't able to have the conservations I had envisioned. Our discussions were sterile and polite. Most of the time, he talked about his political campaign for representative from Sigulu Island in the Ugandan Parliament. He mentioned often that he wanted us to help support him in this endeavor.

Kessy had given her father my manuscript to read while he was with her in North Carolina. He asked if he could to keep it. On Friday morning while we were sitting outside watching the grandchildren play, I asked Otieno what he thought about my story. He looked into my face and said, "Nothing was left out, nothing was added, and everything was true." I don't remember him saying that he was sorry, but I'd like to think that he was. Before he left, he gave me a list of spelling corrections for some of the Swahili words. He didn't seem to be distressed that he had missed out on our children's lives. He didn't mention his other children or anything about his wives. He told me what he was doing on Sigulu Island, and then said that I am still remembered fondly by his family.

The wedding was a beautiful celebration of the circle of love uniting Jesus, Andrea, Otiga and Octavius. I have never seen a more joyful wedding than this one. From the first glance of Andrea, Otiga did not stop smiling. As they stood before God, friends, and family, and shared their vows, their joy was bubbling over. God was the center of this ceremony.

Bruce and I were able to continue the festivity for another week because the bride, groom, and Octavius flew to Orlando with us for their honeymoon. We played with Octavius while Otiga and Andrea began their life together as husband and wife.

Of course, the favorite subject to revisit after we completely dissected the marvelous moments of the wedding was Otieno's visit. We agreed that this had been a wonderful venue for their reunion with him. It was probably less traumatic for everyone because he wasn't center stage all the time. It was good that he had come because he had been a shadow throughout the children's lives, and now he was no longer the missing link.

They now have memories of the time they spent with Otieno and when the images of him grow dim, they have pictures to recharge their recollections and to share with their children.

I began writing my story in July of 1982, but it wasn't until now that I saw the ending. God gave the children and me this beautiful closure by allowing us to say goodbye to Otieno.

The next story to be told will be theirs.

# Acknowledgements

To my Lord Jesus Christ. You are Love. You are my Peace that passes understanding. You are the Joy that is my strength. I am your child. I love You. Thank You for loving me.

To my beautiful friends in Thika, Kenya, who had so little, but shared everything.

To Trudi Kiliru and Jerri Wangia for welcoming me to Thika and for being kind and caring friends.

To David Kungu Kanya, Headmaster at Thika Memorial Church School, for hiring me as a teacher and then forgiving me for leaving my class without warning.

To Susan Habembe; for being my devoted daughter and a faithful sister to the other children. I love you and miss you.

To my loving father, Eugene White, who will remain my hero and my children's hero forever.

To my mother, Mary White, for forgiving me for breaking her heart. and for being a strong and successful role model.

To my children; Melissa, Otiga, and Nekessa, for listening and editing and never telling me to give this dream up, even after thirty years.

To my loving husband, Bruce, you rescued my heart and made it whole.

To June Bemis, for being a friend when I really needed one, and for remaining my friend all these years.

To my brother Fred, who never turned away.

To my brother Graham and his amazing wife, Cathy, for being my balcony people and faithful prayer warriors for our family.

To Dr. Jack Lynd, who welcomed my children and me into the Edgewood Ranch family.

To Dr. Joan Consolver, who hired me as a teacher and then remained my friend for life.

To Twila Papay, Professor of English and Writing at Rollins College, Winter Park Fl, for her encouragement and guidance in class, and for the blessing of her friendship

To Joseph Papay, for lovingly editing my original manuscript.

To Wally White, an amazing author, a dynamic man of God, and a constant encourager and editorial advisor.

To Irene Heatherington, my dear friend and advisor for life.

To Lynn and Earl Hotalen, and Lisa and Stuart Eldridge, who remain faithful examples of God's Love to everyone who comes to Edgewood Children's Ranch.

To Jennifer Weagraff and all her family, Dana Anderson, Melissa, Lisa Eldridge, Josh Squires, Mike Armbruster, Gayla Page, The Forresters, Gerogia Holmes, Andrea, Sarah and Mike Watters, Josh and Sara White, the dedicated staff of Edgewood, and other wonderful Social Media experts who will encourage friends to read *Escape Under the Kenyan Moon,* Thank You.

To Edgewood Children's Ranch in Orlando, Fl, for being a loving and safe place for children to grow strong, as they discover the love of Jesus.

# Word List

Abaluhya- (Ah-bah-**loo**-yah) The language spoken by the Luhya tribe. The language spoken on Sigulu Island.. (The Luhya also Luhya or, **Abaluhya**) are the second largest ethnic group in Kenya, numbering about 5.3 million people, or 14% of Kenyan population. The words Luhya and Abaluhya are interchangeable for either the tribe or the language.

Akinyi- (Ah-**kin**-yee) Widow of Otieno's brother, Otiga, "inherited" by Otieno after Otiga's death. She is the mother of Susan, Peter, and Juliet.

Askari- (ahss-**kar**-ree) Swahili for guard or soldier.

Auma- (Ah-**oo** -mah) Otieno's mother and the first name of our daughter. Auma Nekessa Habembe (nickname Kessy).

Ayah- (ah-yah) A maid or helper.

Busia- ((Boo-see-ah) The area of Kenya near Lake Victoria, general area of the Luhya tribe.

Changaa- (**chahng**-ah) Homemade liquor or moonshine made on the island.

Chania- (**cha**-nee-ah) Name of the waterfall in Thika, Kenya that was the beautiful back-drop for the Blue Post Inn.

Chapati- (cha-**pah** -tee) Swahili for a flat, fried bread that is enjoyed with the meal or with tea.

Duka- (**doo**-kah) Swahili for store or shop

Duka Moja~ (**Doo**-kah **Moh**-Jah) Swahili. One of the popular shops in Thika. It was a grocery/ general store.

Jiko~ (**ghee**-koh) A small charcoal type grill used by many as their only stove.

Imani~ (Ee-**mah**-nee) Name of the company school in Thika.

Jambo Sana~ (jahm-boh-**sah**-nah) Swahili for good day. A general anytime greeting.

Jogo Kamakia~ (**Joh**-goh Kah-**mah**-kee-ah) Name of the apartment complex we lived in for a few months in Thika.

Jangola Kwach~ (Jun-**go**-lah Kwahch) Abaluhya. Otieno's nickname for Otiga meaning fierce leopard.

Kanga~ (kahn-gah) A brightly colored piece of cloth worn by many of the native women as a skirt or dress, or a wrap used to hold a baby on the mother's back

Kenya~ (Ken-yah) A country in East Africa.

Kikuyu~ (Kih-**koo**-yoo) A tribe in Kenya. Many Africans in Thika were from this tribe.

Lake Victoria ~ Large Lake bordered by Kenya ,Uganda and Tanzania. Sigulu Island is in Lake Victoria.

Luhya~ (**Loo**-yah) A tribe in East Africa. Otieno was Luhya. The Luhya (also Luyia,Abaluhya) are the second largest ethnic group in Kenya, numbering about 5.3 million people, or 14% of Kenyans. The words Luhya and Abaluhya are interchangeable for either the tribe or the language.

Matatu~ (**mah**-tah-too) Swahili for "taxi". Used primarily by the Africans.

Musungu- (moo-**soon**-goo) Possibly Swahili. Means "foreigner" or "white person"

Muzuri Sana- (mm-**zoo**-ree sah-nah) Swahili for "thank you."

Nairobi- (Ni-**roh**-bee) Capital of Kenya

Ngotami (Nn-go-**tah**-mee) Name of Otieno's grandfather

Omo- (Oh-moh) Brand name of the only detergent sold in Thika at the time we were there..

Otiga Habembe- (Oh-**tee**-gah Hah-**bem**- bay) Abaluhya. Name of Otieno's and my son

Pascal- (Pass-**cal**) Otieno's older brother. Chief of the village when I was there with Otieno.

Sukuma-wiki- ( soo-**koo**-me **wee**-kee) Dish of boiled greens, part of the daily meal of many Africans in the area.

Thika- (**Thee**-kah) City where we lived in Kenya, located just north of Nairobi.

Ugali-(oo-**gah**-lee) A stiff porridge made by boiling corn or cassava flour in water. Then torn off pieces are dunked into the sukuma-wiki broth and eaten.

# Pictures From Then and Now

Otieno holding his two favorite possessions; his African fly whisk and his diploma from Ohio State University.

Otiga is practicing to be a chief. His father bought him his own African fly whisk, but I think Otiga smiles too much to ever be a chief.

Otiga, Nekessa, and I are in the living room of our stone house on the Thika Memorial School compound. We used the fireplace occasionally during June, July, and August, which was the cold and wet season.

Melissa is at school in her Imani uniform.
She was in third position in her class ranking.

Susan, Otiga, Peter, Melissa, Nekessa, and Juliet are in our living room in the stone house. It was nice that our furniture finally arrived from the States. It looked right at home on the red cement floors. The strange looking white rectangle on the left side of the picture is the sliding door that separated the dining room from the living room.

Otiga, Peter and Melissa enjoying the school playground after hours. The red clay dirt was nice during the dry season, but it became a sea of moving red mud during the rainy season. My class was in the wooden building. The windows had no glass, so during the rains, our room stayed cold, wet and muddy.

The front of our house faced the school. It was wonderful having our home, the school, and the church so close to each Other.

This is Bruce and me, twenty-some years ago in Italy at Epcot in Orlando, FL. We actually went to Italy a few years ago, but we are younger and thinner in this picture.

This beautiful picture of Melissa, Otiga, and Nekessa was taken at Andrea and Otiga's wedding on July 17, 2010.

# Author's Address

I didn't actually decide to write this book. The story was in me, demanding to be released, much like a child ready to be born. The memories swelled within my mind, until they could no longer be contained. As the words poured out, my pen raced across the paper, trying to keep up with my thoughts.

Also like a child, *Escape Under the Kenyan Moon* has taken many years to mature. I started writing it in July of 1982, just a few months after we had returned to America. The original title was *Rock Me Gently*, from the song "Rock Me Gently," but that suggested the story was about Otieno.

The next title was *Askari* which means guard in Swahili, because God guarded and rescued us. However, this title did not let the reader know what the story was about.

The title, *Escape Under the Kenyan Moon,* came into being while our family was together during the Christmas holiday in 2011. We had so much fun as we all sat around the kitchen table, late into the night, throwing out ideas to be considered. We all agreed on *Escape Under the Kenyan Moon.* I don't know if it was the best title, or we were just too sleepy to continue. .

*Escape Under the Kenyan Moon* is about God's unfailing love. I know that I will never fully comprehend all the ways He protected my children and me in this tropical paradise that turned dark and frightening. I believe God didn't calm the storm during this time, but He led us through it, so we would understand that we could trust Him during the trials of life that were yet to come.

I would love to hear from you, and to know if my story related to you in your life's journey.

Email Address:
**carole.askari@gmail.com**

Carole Myrick
PO Box 616278
Orlando, FL 32861

Made in the USA
Charleston, SC
18 March 2014